Ein ♡ kann man nicht ka..!
doch wenn man flie..
bekommt man ein..

BEST POETS OF 2016

VOL. 1

Zur Erinnerung an Deine
Tante Lisa
(Margarete Lisa Flatebo)

John T. Eber Sr.
MANAGING EDITOR

A publication of

Eber & Wein Publishing
Pennsylvania

Library of Congress
Cataloging in Publication Data

ISBN 978-1-60880-571-6

Proudly manufactured in the United States of America by

Eber & Wein Publishing
Pennsylvania

In Praise of Excellence:
M. M. Ryan's "The Offering"

A commentary by Grace Cavalieri

A truly great poem has natural strength—a text with meanings to be discerned, line after line—but more than that, feelings, rooted in the reality of the story. A good poem is one I read carefully because there's charisma that comes from its fullness and sincerity. M. M. Ryan's poem "The Offering" has everything we want in free verse. She couldn't possibly have accomplished this poem if she'd been tied to a rocking chair using rhyme, forced to twist words to fit meaning, making her a prisoner of metrics. Instead, we have a structured, flowing narrative, which tells a fascinating story.

Ryan begins beautifully by letting imagination enter the poem, "I imagine her sitting, palm over palm..." and then she creates a character—so here the poet becomes a playwright, making up a character to create situation. The poet puts her character "...on a train / Or maybe a bus...." Next we have the sensual sound of the wheels and the motion of arrival to a new place. I love the way Ryan can start a line with an action word "...clasping a single suitcase...." Action words (gerunds) are motion lotion, and they make us move our eyes to the next word, then the next line. The writer even dresses her character so we can fully see her. This is the magic of imagery where every visual element is accounted for. The poet also gives us a tone of weather in the poem, "...the air holds traces of green warmth, / or maybe winter's bite holds..." (I love 'winter's bite'). Then the plot thickens to a relationship, and we see why our character has been sent on this unexpected journey. Always, the poet uses the art of simile and metaphor throughout: "...the dead boy's uncle whips his barbed tongue...." At the end of the poem the speaker (the teller of the story) allows her mind to wander again back into the imagined world. "I wonder if she felt old enough for her crucifixion...." Then the speaker enters the poem's landscape. Never before has the speaker been in the landscape; Ryan lets the drama play without intrusion. The poem ends, "... I do not ask questions, / But spend a lifetime listening." What a beautiful way to bring the poem home.

The power of poetry is a matter of focus. Can the poet hold our attention for ten, twenty, thirty lines? Ryan can, for she has character, situation, plot, and mystery. Also there's a psychological spiraling of emotions from beginning to end. This is essential—something to see, hear, smell, or taste. Sensuality!

Why send a poem out into the world deaf, dumb, and blind? This poet knows what sustains us in the reading.

What kind of risk does the poet take? What does she have to overcome? Well first she has to trust that the reader will read slowly, and will read every line, because the beauty of this piece is that every line depends on the one before it and the one after.

This is "super power poetry" that shows Ryan has a well-developed skill set, because her line lengths show just the way to read it. Ryan begins the poem with a long line, "I imagine her sitting, palm of her palm, on a train..." then she contracts it in line 2, "Or maybe a bus...." Here we have an expansion followed by a contraction. This is breathing! The poem becomes a living, breathing thing. Expansion plus contraction equals breath.

The narrative is critical because it's a story, and so we want a beginning, middle, and an end, but more than that, we want emotions connecting to the words. We also want accuracy. There's not one lump under the lines here. Every word is the right word in the right order. Here's where I praise blank verse or free verse. Had Ryan been tied to a rocking chair rhyme she couldn't have had language to tell the tale.

What I like most about this poem is the vulnerability and the courage to tell it. All of us can use language but a true writer tells her truth; and in chasing the melody, we find a living experience on the page.

Grace Cavalieri is the founder and producer of "The Poet and the Poem" on public radio, now celebrating forty years on-air. Her latest book A Memoir Live Upon the Wicked Stage *is available on Amazon (newacademia/scarith). www.gracecavalieri.com*

Soliloquy

Alone in contemplation
Alone in discourse
Thoughts adrift in the openness
In the underneath of a somber sky
Cries come from the wilderness
Tumbling rumbles grumble
And roll in from the nether
Soft lazy spatters
Kiss the weeping terrain
Tiny staccato callings
Sound out their greetings
Chattering in conversation
Lonesome tweets of song
Join in a celebration of wings
As stoic palms and pines
Stand in majestic patience
Serenity hovers in harmony
With a stillness of sublimity
All alone with compassion
I am mesmerized yet composed
I follow their pleasures
As they hide in mine
Reflections dance in glee
In a gracious reverent reverie
Alone in the presence of being
Alone in this moment in time

James L. Harter
Palm Coast, FL

Seasons

Where to begin?
Spring, summer, fall, winter

All seasons blend one to the other.
Spring, slowly, softly a hint of a warm breeze,
It brings the magic of life renewed!
Gentle rain, sunny days,
Life springing from barren earth—
Seeds dropped in the ground—
Trees once again in their dresses of green.
Birds singing, flowers blooming!

Summer tip-toeing in a time of growth
Ripening, moving onward to harvest time
Fall arrives, clear blue skies, crisp mornings,
Frosty nights, leaves falling—a soft blanket
Of color: red, yellow and green

Winter creeps in—a blanket of snow—
A time for all things large and small to rest,
To sleep under your blanket of snow.

Until spring, so go the seasons!

Josephine Ingalls
New Smyrna, FL

Ghost Tales

Our mountain way of life
was like no other.
When someone was in need
nearby there was always a brother.
Neighbors shared with neighbors
in every way they could.
When winter winds began to blow
everybody helped gather in firewood.
Before long, snow began to fall.
We could hear the cold wind wail.
At night we all sat around the fireplace.
Listen! Dad is telling a big ghost tale.
I snuggled up closer to the fire
until my front side began to burn.
As hotter and hotter I got
my back side I had to turn.
We all sat and listened to ghost tales
until the fire turned to embers.
I ran to bed as fast as I could.
Dad's ghost tales gave me the tremors.
I pulled the cover up over my head
and shut my eyes real tight.
I was afraid a big ghost would get me
and carry me off into the night.

Mary Carr
Sevierville, TN

My poem was inspired while listening to my husband reminisce about his childhood. He was born in a mountain community called The Sugarlands. It became an official part of the Great Smoky Mountain National Park in 1934 when he was five years old. He remembers his dad holding everyone spellbound and scared of the dark after they listened to his ghost tales. Soon after, congress approved the full establishment of the park, and the families began moving away. My husband's family was the last family to move from their Tennessee mountain home when he was thirteen years old.

The Joys of Spring

When the mockin' bird is singin'
And the air is filled with spring
And the daffodils are bloomin'
And the swallows on the wing,
Well, it's then my heart is gladdened
By the sights and sounds I love
After winter's brought me shivers
And the snows from up above.
How I love to hear the croakin'
Of the happy little frogs
And the chatter of the sparrows
And the barkin' of the dogs.
All of nature has awakened
From the warmin' of the sun
And I'm thankin' the creator
For an awesome job well done.

Larry Sabiston
Worthington, IN

New Dimension

Sun radiantly rising, campfire burning,
   trees whispering all around,
    fish dancing on top of the lake.
Birds chirping.
In the distance the waves are rolling in
   from a quiet sea.
What a beautiful way to start your day.
Each day will be different,
a new challenge to face.
Take one day at a time.
Believe in a Higher power.
Keep your mind open,
talk to your Higher power;
you will get over the hurdle.
Let go of your worries, fears,
and resentments. Give it to your Higher power.
Help others.
Make amends when you can.
You will be amazed.
Your eyes will open
to the peace and serenity of life,
dolphins dancing afar.

Ralph Canfield
Wapato, WA

The Whispering Wind

A warm Santa Ana wind felt like a father's caress
On the nape of our necks
On a warm LA day
Causing us to perspire
And the winds kicked up mini dust cyclones on the beach at sunset
Misting with our perspiration and foam from the sea making
prisms
And rainbows on our skin
Even the kingfish watching over us
With its rainbow plumage was pleased
Ever reminding us of the Creator's given life
And the brotherhood and sisterhood that bonds us
The kingfisher is happy with God's Creation

Gavin J. Wahl
Long Beach, CA

The Rosary

Many Catholics the Rosary still pray.
Ancient Creed sure prepares well the way.
  Six "Lord's Prayer," "Glory Be,"
  "Ave" count: fifty-three;
End with "Hail, Holy Queen"—faith display!

Joyful Mysteries provide glad sensation—
Angel's "Ave," to Liz visitation,
  Christ's birth in Bethlehem,
  Jesus' bar-mitzvah mirth;
Father's business spurs Mom's contemplation.

The five Sorrowful Mysteries are sad—
"Let not My will but Thine be done, Dad,"
  The cruel scourging, throne crown,
  Thrice with cross falling down;
Crucifixion and death seemed so rad!

Glorious Mysteries God's glory project—
Resurrection, Ascension direct,
  The descent of the Spirit,
  The Assumption, let's cheer it;
Coronation brings Mary respect.

The five Luminous Mysteries are new—
Christ baptized, Cana's miracle, too,
  "Not this world" proclamation,
  Bright white Transfiguration,
Holy Eucharist with Christ's presence true!

Dennis G. Johnston
Spokane, WA

With God

Happy for the better times we spent.
Even more, for the given love we meant.
Forgiven by the Begotten Son He sent.
Rest now, you're finally home —
With God!

William H. Collins
Binghamton, NY

I wrote this poem for my friend, who had taken care of her ninety-three-year-old father with Alzheimer's for seven years and finally lost him in the nursing home where she had sent 750 letters and cards — one each day to express her love. She was so distraught that I told her I would like to write one last card to him from her to place in his coffin. She thanked me and said, "It says it all," and cried. This let the pain out and let the love in as God intended.

E Pluribus Unum

How did we get
  from no need to lock doors,
and the old corner stores,
  from affordable fun,
to such fear of the gun?
From "till death do us part,
to news ripping our heart?
From happy with need
  to abominable greed?
From respect from our foes
  to now John and Jane Doe?
  Together we will
climb back up that hill.
Our basics are strong,
and our patience is long.
We still care about tired,
  hungry and poor,
our youth and our pets,
The old couple next door.
We'll cart over soup
  and sit on the stoop
to talk about ways
  to bring light through the haze.
Movers and solvers —
  it's just what we do —
  Americans true.

Joyce Walker-Bruce
Prospect Park, PA

Grandma's Advice

Life is so short…
    but don't break the rules!
People who do that
    just look like they're fools.

Bestow lots of praises.
    Be quick to forgive!
Offering help where it's needed
    is the way we should live.

Just practice these things
    for your own happiness!
You'll keep love in your life…
    and you'll be very blessed!

Marilyn C. Van Patten
Elkhart, IN

Here's this old eighty-seven-year-old woman who's been exercising her poetry pen again! My calendar always points out about 135 names on dates of birthdays and anniversaries every year. Each card I send gets the new yearly poem I've written that's different than last year's. (They contain lots of stickers that pertain to the poem theme too!) Many of my friends call to thank me and tell me how much they enjoy my poetry! (Some of them call it my "mission.") Makes me happy too! It's my very favorite thing to do. I love it!

In the Dark

...and pray for those
victims of tragic events

For more than two thousand years,
every year, for the other
three hundred and thirteen days,
the pews remain empty:
unused prayer places;
while Christ,
ever continuously hanging in the dark,
alone,
wounded,
suffering,
almost completely abandoned,
waits for all humanity to appear:
knowing that practically
none
of his children
care to come,
will to come,
want to come.

Charles O. Rand
Springerville, AZ

*I am a seventy-seven-year-old, retired juvenile probation officer from
San Francisco, CA. My wife of fifty-two years, Cristina, and I, live in
Springerville, AZ where I am uncovering a prehistoric Indian ruin. Come
and join those interested—no education or experience necessary, only an
honest desire to learn from the past. It is exciting to learn that the people
who built it have always been here, not the Anasazi—ancient strangers,
the Hohokam—all gone, the Sinagua—without water or any others with
made-up names. My teacher doesn't agree. Only the descendants do.*

Violets

I used to gather the little violets
    For my loving mother dear.
I would search the tiny spots,
    Along the paths, both far and near.

A precious little blossom,
    A jewel within my eyes,
To take my loving mother,
    Who now within her grave lies.

They said when she was living,
    Of the flowers she loved the best,
She always chose the little violets
    From all the ones you might suggest.

Now that she is in the Kingdom
    Where the flowers always bloom,
I hope the violets may be blooming
    Just outside the mansion's room.

Clinton E. Riddle
Sweetwater, TN

Do We Hear?

We fight and curse,
But do we converse?
Terror and fear,
Do we hear?
Do we listen to what
another has to say
On this sad, tumultuous day?
Bring back calm and peace
And sweet release,
No shooting or bomb
But constant peace
Or many more will die,
And we will wonder *why*.
With our cell phones
tethered to our ears,
Do we hear?

Janice R. Meyer
St. Louis, MO

The Alphabet

The alphabet is a wonderful thing
It holds all the letters
It can be compared to the wishing well
Without walls, boundaries, or fetters
And from within one can draw out
A peck of pleasure and joy
Why anyone with a simple idea
Can create a wonderful story
It all starts out with the letter "A"
Amazing as that can be
Plus all the other letters involved
To keep it company
If we didn't have the alphabet
Can you imagine how boring life would be
Because everyone knows without A, B and C
There would be no Y, O, U, nor M and E…

Robert E. Brock
Hampton, VA

The Thread

The room rakes of silence, and I look around with painful eyes, that burn

my soul. I mourn, my heart is hollow.

For I have lost too many to death. The echoes of their laughter are but pin drops in my blood, and I am forgetting their ways, they are but shadows in me.

For I have grown cold like a fire with no warmer. There are only the colors of darkness where they once lived.

For I am empty because I cannot touch what my heart has felt. Their spirits linger in my soul like beautiful flowers that cannot be touched nor smelled. Yet their memories still fight to creep from within me.

I rest my head upon my pillow tarnished with many tears, hungry for them.

There is an open window beside my bed and a breeze of wind blows gently and nests upon my tears. I looked down upon my bed and there is but a single bit of thread ever so small. I saw it move with the help of the wind. Then I felt my heart and felt it beat and I knew they still live within me.

Their memories cling like dancing shadows in my heart and linger in my soul like an open Xmas pageant in July.

Rena Kennebrew
Pomona, CA

The Debtor

My life is now bills, bills, bills.
I'm ready to head for the hills.
Think I'll go to Vegas and bet,
playing blackjack and roulette!
I'll be a real lucky so and so
when I win a pot of dough
and I can pay off credit card debt!
That will make me happy, you bet!
Life is a gamble, they say
and I've found it true.
But beating the odds we can do
when our Vegas dreams come true.
Viva Las Vegas!

Jacqueline Susan Stone
Cottonwood, CA

Fathers

F—is for the million of things that he has done for us.
A—is for the awesome times that we've had
T—is for the tender love that he's given
H—is for all of his helpful advice
E—is for all of his everlasting love
R—is for the right words—laughter

A father's job may not be done for a long time, and his
job is never done.

Diana G. Woodsum
Auburn, ME

The Voice of a Poem

When the voice of a poem
Speaks lovely and gently heals, mends, repairs.
How it marvelously rewinds and re-mantels
The brokenhearted with high expectations,
With auspices of faith and hope,
With strings of violins with sonatas of love,
Yea, so endearing as streams, cool and refreshing,
As if shedding tons of feeling upon the senses,
As then, ah! As a breath of air lifts life,
A miracle touches the heart, the mind, the soul,
And life begins and lives again.

Yea! As the voice of a poem cometh forth,
With an entourage of repertoire enlightens so,
Yea, as sweet nectar nurtures, caressing the heart,
The mind, the soul, soothing and calming,
With such delicacies, as such favorable delights,
As resonance with horizons of dreams,
Coming as blessings from above,
Streaming down upon my soul,
Embracing me forever, emphatically!
Shall be sealed, with His eternal love.

Elena V. Rivera Diaz
Tampa, FL

Disappointment

How does disappointment come?
In gushing tears? In anger subdued?
In wantonness, fears? Or an uncaring attitude?
Be it a hasty word, a friend's distress,
A rumor heard, a loneliness.
A broken vow, a sudden stress,
Deceit somehow or forgetfulness.
Disappointment will be close for those who care the most,
Who risk and reach and strive to teach.
Who patiently wait and agitate for change.
To touch the hurting and needy,
The poor and the greedy,
The forlorn and helpless,
Serving the world's hopeless.
Disappointments come to every tribe and race,
To rich and poor from shore to shore.

Jane P. KenKnight
Cincinnati, OH

I wrote this poem while thinking about all the people that are being killed by terrorists in our cities and throughout the world. There is much pain!

Darling Lisa

"It's a done deal," dear Lisa exclaims,
A phrase picked up from her mom Elaine.
It's one of her favorite exclamations,
which she often utters with exhilaration.
Though her vocabulary not very extensive,
Her spirit and grit is very intensive.
Down syndrome has given her much to overcome,
But that didn't stop her from attending her prom.
She's adamant about her music selection,
And now has an eclectic collection.
As for dancing she has natural rhythm;
It springs from somewhere within.
Her most favorite game is Candyland,
Which I play with her whenever I can.
Her favorite character is The Incredible Hulk;
She loves his greeness, his strength, and bulk.
Her life has been nothing short of a miracle,
Not always easy and ofttimes difficult.
When an organ transplant became imperative,
Her dad's donation was the altruistic alternative.
It was viable for some twenty years,
When dialysis became abundantly clear.
Some days for her are better than others,
And the tough ones she somehow weathers.
I can truly ascertain
That we have entertained an angel unawares.

Hilda Hanze
Ossining, NY

Everlasting

God, so I learned in Sunday school,
Is an angry old man in the sky.
That image stalked me like a shadow
And bent me in pain for all of my years
Until that bright blessed morning
When a sunbeam
Burst through my soul's shuttered window
And kissed me awake from that dream.
God, that kiss told me,
Is all of the heavens,
Every sun, moon, and star.
God moves through everything living
Flowing like breath,
And therefore, I, too, am God
Having an adventure:
God laughing, crying, singing, mourning,
God winning, God failing,
God at home in the castle
As well as homeless on the street.
God dances, makes love,
Gives birth, sleeps,
Weaving through newborn dawn
Into the ancient night and back again,
Everlasting.

Diane Crawford
Selden, NY

My Ride of Pride

When I received my badge as a registered nurse, I was so proud.
In England, we had no graduation ceremony. Just a letter. No crowd.
Then when I obtained my Visa to enter this great land,
I read and re-read that coveted paper clutched in my hand.
The man I loved, loved me too. I was so proud. We were betrothed.
On the day we married, my happiness and pride found new growth.
Then children were born — more pride. As if we alone were able!
Other infants could not compare to those rocked in our cradle.
Years went by. Numerous days of great pride were known.
At school, academic, sports and musical abilities, by each,
were shown,
But nothing prepared me for the pride of every family member there,
When my first grandson finished boot camp, an answer to his prayer.
I was so proud! Just wish Grandpa could have shared that
special day.
He was in all our hearts, and there will always stay, I pray.
Adam survived the Crucible, on the way to fulfill his dream
with four hundred others, smartly at attention (I cried with pride).
As he then became, forever a United States Marine!

Elsie Stowell Raymond
Roseville, CA

*I was born in England, and my mother was in the hospital from when I was three.
I planned to be a nurse so I could bring her home but was not able to, though
eventually I became an RN. She died in a mental hospital after twenty-nine years
as a patient. I left school at fourteen and worked six years (all of World War II)
as a civil nursing reserve. Then from 1945 to 1948, I trained finally to be an RN.
I've completed over fifty years as a nurse for others' mothers. I emigrated to my
mother's homeland, America, in 1948.*

My Wonderful Aunt Alice

I have an amazing aunt who means the world to me;
My love for her stretches far away, as far as I can see.

She was always there for me whenever times were bad,
Like when my mom was so very sick and I felt really sad.

She made clothes for my dollies; they were oh, so nice.
I felt so very lucky… it was just like paradise!

I'd get packages in the mail full of exciting things.
It was so fun to open them; it made me jump and sing.

My mother had cancer most of the years of my life;
Looking back I remember much sorrow and strife.

But Aunt Alice would come quite often and visit all of us.
I remember going downtown and riding on the bus.

We went shopping and she bought me some fabric to sew.
I made my first blouse and I was extra proud, you know.

Going off to college, she gave me a special present:
Navy and lime-green towels; oh, they were heaven sent!

She came here for my wedding; it meant so much to me
To have her serve the cake and punch for John and me.

When I was lucky enough to have my own two sons,
She was always there to play games; oh, such fun!

I'm grateful to have such a wonderful aunt and confidant.
I wish everyone could have such a treasured aunt!

Nancy L. Oswald
Gladstone, OR

The Mighty Oak

Look upon this colossal stalwart oak,
branches stretch forth in a twisted reach.
Embracing wisdom far beyond the decades,
share not but deep within its soul.
Compassion extends to all that land,
or need a place to rest.
He's held his station for a hundred years,
and will stand for a hundred more
as forceful gusts try their best
to break upon a limb.
His stupendous endurance will outweigh,
Mother Nature's relentless sabotage,
Yet tender to the thriving hive
that occupy a spray.
With roots that expand the circumference of leaves,
drink of this thirsty acreage.
As Spring sheds joyful tears,
bring forth another ring of maturity
held fast by the passion of a vanishing day,
watching as the sun retreats beyond
the vivacious horizon.

Joann C. Martinez
Concord, CA

Sweet as an Angel

When I first gazed upon your beauty,
  My heart was filled with warmth;
And your eyes were like no other I've seen,
  And your smile was as warm as the sun.

As we speak, your voice is so soft and sweet,
  Your skin as smooth as silk.
Everything about you is unique;
  You are something to cherish and hold.

You always make me feel good when you're around,
  For whosoever loves you is lucky;
They will always be surrounded in your beauty,
  Their life full of joy and happiness.

Once again I've seen your beauty at its most,
  Warm and wonderful at its fullest moment,
The smile, the touch, and happiness,
  All that is within you and only you an angel.

Rudolph Ramsey Jr.
San Antonio, TX

God's Love

God loves me with a significant love;
He made me in His image.

God loves me with an everlasting love;
He gave His Son to be my sacrifice
So eternity with Him is mine.

God loves me with an abundant love;
He provides all my needs.

God loves me with a love of touch;
Jesus became flesh to live among us.

I don't always feel or sense or know this love,
But it is there for me!

I must open the portals of my heart
And let it in!

Myrt Offutt
Hot Springs, AR

Some Days

Some days life seems fair,
Because we have someone who really cares.
Some days life seems so hard,
Because of circumstances unexplained.
Some days with so much going on in public news,
We feel that we really are so confused.
How do we right the wrong in this world?
We open our hearts
And begin to pray.
God, please grant us another day
Of love, praise, and good cheer
For our families and friends
That are so dear.

Mary G. Garner-Atkins
Suffolk, VA

Reading

Be taught early how to read
It answers many questions
about the past and future views
plus today's changing patterns
Yesterday may be forgotten
Today is very real
The future seems foreboding
but reading fills the bill
and gives the truthful answers
which is a daily yearning
because one keeps on learning!

Juanita Weber
Florissant, MO

Starlight

You are the starlight
That brightens the night,
The star that shines
In the dark, dark night.

The face in the moon
Reminds me of you,
Keeps me in tune
In the dark, dark night.

Betty R. Patterson
Goshen, IN

Sonnet to Fiction

Yes, that second time I crossed near your store
Of fresh pies and sweet rolls, the scent from all
Those pastries jellied, glazed, and delicate
To the nth degree tempting youth's desires.
Then you caught my gaze through the wide glass door
And I gasped. Now beyond my parents' wall
I would not be denied guilt. I shoved it
Down into my sub-conscience where choirs

Silently sing of cravings. Hankerings
On distinct nights. Revered by sure crowds. Men.
Butchers, bakers, and candlestick makers. But me still wary
I entered your shop. With a piqued grin you
Patiently answered my concocted questions;
You sensed correctly that I was looking for no library.

Jeffery Moser
Aurora, CO

Thank You, Majestic Birds

Look at the turkey vulture as it soars
Up in God's great big outdoors
Coming into the trees to rest once more
From cleaning up the earth's yucky gore.

Sara Bussom
Carlisle, PA

Gray Days

Stark, damp, and gray days wane in cold darkness.
Memories of days past keep thoughts of present near.
Forging forth the realization of time,
Past and present signs show sadness and wonder.
Streams of hope beckon us.
Life's path crosses unpromising waters.
Pain and hardship prevail.
Understanding of oneself is most important,
Achieving new heights of compromise and love.

Ellen A. Gaskey-Berryman
Virginia Beach, VA

Keep working toward the goals you have set for yourself and like who you see in the mirror.

Baby Gifts 1923

A hat, sweater matching booties to
Some belly bands to keep the navel clean.
And you can bet a dress or two hand stitched.

Bird's I dapper homemade, to be washed every day.
Homemade blankets, baby bottle nipples
A dish, a bent-handle spoon.

A cradle, rock back and forth — to help the baby sleep;
You see, five girls and boys took their turn rocking the cradle
While Mother cooked, over a hot black stove.
A long dress, apron too.
A child's arms around her leg to keep warm.
High black button shoes, midwife earned $10 per month;
Doctor stuck in mud: $20.00.

Jenie A. Clark
Belmont, ME

Simple Pleasures

Take time to enjoy simple pleasures.
God gives us many awesome treasures.
Like when a cardinal comes to feed
at the bird feeder with the sunflower seed
or the hummingbird as he soars around
till at last a sweet, cool drink he has found.

I watch a gentle dove in the tall tree.
(I believe she is really watching me.)
A dark blue jay I hear singing nearby —
way up in the tall tree so very high.
Take time to enjoy simple pleasures.
God gives us many awesome treasures.

Flowers of every shape with colors so bright
Only God can paint them just right.
The green of grass and trees He colors for all —
to be enjoyed by us, young, old, or small.
Take time to enjoy these simple pleasures.
God gives us so many awesome treasures.

Elsie M. Lehmann
New Braunfels, TX

A Coat of Love

Bought at a secondhand store
Worn by many
The color was bright
The price was right
By a mother, newly widowed
On a budget that was tight

What did it matter if it had a patch
Or the buttons did not match
The lining was thick and tightly attached
It would keep her child warm in the winter

They laughed at her when she walked by
Even made her cry
She suddenly realized
She no longer belonged
With those who had more
Or families with fathers

A frigid storm blew in
It chilled them to the marrow
They began to shiver and shake
In their flimsy new coats
Hers kept her warm as toast

She did not mean to gloat
As she walked by in her patched coat
She was filled with a new pride
That she did not hide
She knew her wealth came from
A mother's love and the warmth of her coat.

Ann Marie Bernstine
Summerfield, FL

Untitled

A song to Jesus
　and anybody
on the outskirts of Heaven
I want to live
　on the outskirts of Heaven
where the skies are always blue,
　the grass is green,
and I can see
　fish swimming in the river.
I want to live
　on the outskirts of Heaven
where people are loving,
where people never fight,
where people do what is right.
I want to live
　on the outskirts of Heaven
　with you —
　　forever and ever
　　all right...
Amen

Eleanor A. Tingelstad
Fergus Falls, MN

A New Day

When you wake up in the morning, aren't you glad to be alive!
Don't you feel a keen excitement as you watch the sun arrive?
Think of all the glorious wonders that this day might soon unveil—
Wonder what today will bring me, wonder where my ship will sail.

Why is it that we look forward to the coming of each day,
Eagerly anticipating good things that might come our way?
Every morning seems a challenge, and as each new hour unfolds
We are counting every minute, searching for what this day holds.

Will it be an extra good day? Will my special dreams come true?
It may be that God will grant a day all filled with something new,
But if not, I'll keep on dreaming and remembering as I pray,
Though I don't know what it holds, tomorrow is another day.

Marianne Y. Gordon
Hernando, MS

Rain on Hostas

It is raining on the hostas
in my yard and on the
rabbits who hide under the
broad leaves nibbling
their impromptu umbrellas
while huddled together in the cold,
sitting perfectly, soundlessly,
shivering in fear of
being discovered
by the cat,
who waits under
the porch awning
with its silent, surveying eyes
and occasionally twitching
tail, which catches and
refracts the light
as it arcs back and forth.
And it is raining
while my mother sits
in her rocking chair
gazing out the window,
like the rabbits hiding
under the hostas,
waiting for the rain
to stop so she can
escape her demons.

Annette Gagliardi
Minneapolis, MN

God's Artistic Handiwork

My eyes traverse around me with passion and thankfulness
For all the creations that beautify this place.
The colors, the shapes, the sounds, and the atmosphere —
My heart can't totally express the pleasure, oh, I revere.

Look at the sunshine, see its light, and feel its warmth.
Look at the flowers, single out their colors and their fragrance.
Have you heard the birds, the bees, and the butterflies?
What more have you run into that raptures your smile?

The blue sky with white clouds and silky rainbow rays
The clear blue sea with myriads of seaweeds, sea shells, and fish
The change of seasons that gives us so many ways to relish
God's love, compassion, purity and holiness.

The moment I stepped in this midst of God's handiwork
My soul leaped with joy, my being just esteemed
With gratefulness my life can't totally explain
What an overwhelming creativeness, is this a dream?

Heavenly Father, gift me with Your artistic obsession
So I can share Your passion and love to all Your creations
That You would be seen and appreciated with fervor,
Not just a blessing but an existence of exaltation!

Adelfa G. Lorilla
Seagoville, TX

I have a master's degree in English and am presently retired. Having the opportunity to express my heart's appreciation for God's creations and just being grateful to Him for where we are, what we are, and how we are in this world is a real blessing from the Lord! Gifting me with a very loving husband (Ricardo M. Lorilla) and eight wonderful, God-loving and God-fearing children (Karen, Jan, Zheena, Andrei, Armi, May, Ric, and Jesse) is a great favor from Him. To God be the glory!

A Rapper's Cry

I'm from the *hood*...
　　Life ain't no damn good
Every day the same
　　Trouble daily came.
Hate the hurt and squalor
　　Will I see tomorrow?
I'm in a *lion's den*
　　Being abused by men
Worse than animals they prey
　　Will I see another day?
Guns and knives do hurt
　　Some sick guy went berserk
Cut me bad and deep
　　Robbed me in my sleep
My young blood runs red
　　Is my body dead?
I can't turn around
　　Drugs still have me bound
It's a *one-way street*
　　Where the *devil meets*
Forced to *evil fun*!
　　Children, victims young
In dark *alleys* long
　　Where all *trash* is flung!
Much too weak to run...
　　Mama, forgive your son.

Caecilia DiMartino
Ocala, FL

My friends call me Lillie. I was born and schooled in Linz, Austria and am a survivor of the Second World War. I married a boy from Brooklyn, NY, in 1950, Augustino DiMartino, and I had four children—two girls and two boys, who branched out with seventeen grandchildren. Our tree bears much fruit due to God's divine protection, provision, and abundant blessings. Looking back over my eighty-four years, I recognize the great favor of our loving, heavenly Father—the gifting and talents He allowed to shine in high places that I could have never achieved on my own. Praise God—merci beaucoup Herzlichen Dank sum Vater im Himmel.

God's Love

Don't ride with the
devil but walk with God.
Have faith like the
opening of a pod.
He gave us salvation.
This he freely gave
without any reservation.
God is our heavenly
Father.
This we need to accept
without any bother.
He gave His son to die for
our sins.
He takes away pain and
broken hearts he mends.
Rejoice in God's love;
He sends all His blessings
from above.

Margie R. Chisom
Roanoke, VA

Peace Be with You!

Have a wonderful day!
we tell our friend who takes a walk.
Have fun on your vacation!
we tell the family next door.
Enjoy the concert at the club!
we tell our music-loving sister!

So many wishes, thoughtful and sincere
make friendships glow and grow.
They create memories that last
and echo back to us,
when we hear them spoken by our friends.

Yet... fun and joy and happy thoughts
pertain to present time of life...
Forever, though, I like to say and hear:
Peace be with you!

Aldona Kairys
North Providence, RI

Renewal

Let me paint a picture
Of a quiet summer night:
Gentle breeze is blowing,
Moon is shining bright.
Fireflies are sparkling,
Bird songs all are still.
God has sent this peaceful time
And He always will.

Though it's not a picture
Hanging on the wall,
In your mind you see it
When the chores recall
How desperately you need
To rest and dream and say,
It's renewal time at the end of every day.

Ruth E. Brugler
Burghill, OH

Home Sweet Home

There is a yearning in my soul,
A need to see the things of old.
The ruins of Rome, the Taj Mahal
The pyramids, I'd like it all.
The Tower of London, White Cliffs of Dover
I could gaze at the crown jewels over and over.
The mists of Ireland, the castles of Spain—
To visit them all would be my gain.
Old, old churches, which took centuries to build—
Without tourist they would rarely be filled.
Think of the workmanship, the artisan's skill
They were monuments to God and they're beautiful still.

If the old world I never see
My country has enough beauty to satisfy me.
The snow-capped mountains so steep and tall,
The wondrous colors of a New England fall.
White caps on oceans, waves that roar,
Birds that scatter when waves kiss the shore.
There's so much beauty in this world of ours
From the finest artwork to the plain wildflowers.
So whether or not I ever roam,
America the beautiful is my home sweet home.

Marian W. Brattland
Prior Lake, MN

Today

Each morning before I start my day
I always take time to stop and pray

Today, God, help me to act, to say, and to do
all the things that would be pleasing to You

Today, God, give help to those who are in distress
and give them hope and peace and rest

Today, God, take care of my loved ones far and near
and give them blessings throughout the year

Today, God, bless my homeland I love so dear
and keep America safe from harm and fear

And finally today, I pray that others will clearly see
a reflection of Your love living in me.

Amen

Florace G. Hensley
Titusville, FL

Sow Hate, Reap Votes

Some opposites are equal, others are not,
   like up or down, cold or hot.
One distance that is truly great
   is the one between love and hate.
A proven way for results far above
   gentle appeals for peace and love?
Getting more followers by spewing hate,
   especially if you are a candidate.
Truth is stretched, twisted, and torn,
   reason the object of mindless scorn.
Yet multitudes approve and join the pack,
   like hungry wolves on the attack.
Or perhaps more like the squigjy-man-squee
   that devours itself but continues to be.
Thus haters are often devoured by their hate
   and never return to a less hostile state.

Philip N. Martin
Tulsa, OK

Enigma

There lives a being that is essential
to the perpetuation of life on Earth.
A person who is often diminished
with size and a disrespect of merit.

Others insist that a greater input
provides the strength for survival
and their dominance is essential
to preserve the order of the race.

A more detailed look is needed
to closely probe this question.
One cannot preserve separate
from the other; they must unite.

Sympathy, intuition and beauty
are often characteristic of one.
Others boast strength to provide
protection and security to mates.

As the question of best endures,
the contest seems to end in a tie.
If this conclusion is really true,
oh, why is there still inequality?

Gordon Bangert
Vail, AZ

His Prayer

Lord, strengthen us for the days ahead
These words are in every prayer.
Lord, strengthen us for the days ahead,
A plea for our Father's loving care.

Is there something behind this humble plea
That he does not yet understand?
Does he somehow sense that we may need
A special touch from the Master's hand?

Does he sense there may be a reason for tears,
That the road ahead may be rough?
Behind his calm eyes is there a trace of fear
That our strength may not be enough?

From the depth of my heart I join in his prayer,
Remembering what our Father said:
If we but ask He'll surely grant us
Strength for the day ahead.

What peace to know in the dark of night
When all is done and said,
That his faith was in One who freely gave us
Strength for the days ahead.

Virginia L. Lane
Riegelwood, NC

Awesome!

Like air we rise,
Our world pulled into different directions.
We feel special 'cause we are.
We gather to understand our purpose —
Why we're here.

We have earned our mark —
Like an eagle cleaning his feathers,
Flapping his large wings, sharping his claws —
Always watching for his next prey.

No one knows what tomorrow will bring.
Sometimes the pressure is harder than the solution.
How can we not be together
When we've given each other so much?

Like you, my friend, I failed to feel the passion.
We pushed each other to the brink.
Listening is the key,
The most effective way to help someone.
Now, no one knows that better than I!
It's awesome to know who you are!

John W. Johnson
West Berlin, NJ

The Scene

Look at the fellas who fall at the ground
   Searching and seeking at ahh's around
   Has been trouble and come out before
   Seen looking, standing behind the door

Called inside to meet someone
   Making out by the passing sun
   With fools and such no-nonsense
   Arising back alike such finesse

My, oh my, is she the same as he?
   Breaking beside that same old scene
   As we turn and turn, one once more
   We spent some time as something sure

Now we rest, allotted in time
   Reckoned as past
   No harm alive

Sharon Lewis-Gorrell
Mansfield, OH

Max

We have a little dog;
His name is Max.
To keep him here and well,
We'd gladly pay an income tax.

He was Ray's buddy
Both day and night.
To see them together
Was a pure delight.

Oh, how could we have ever known
The Lord would soon call Ray on home,
To leave a sadness in our hearts,
An empty place of broken parts?

And now this little gentle dog
Stays close to those
Who love him most,
Who care for all his doggie needs,
The best of all the doggie breeds.

Oh, may our Ray look down and smile
That Max is loved and all the while,
Will someday be with him and God
A happy, loving little dog.

Claire Snyder
Sandusky, OH

The reason I wrote this poem was to honor my husband Walter Ray Snyder who passed away April 9, 2016. We have a little sixteen-year-old white dog that spent every minute, day and night, with Ray who adored him. I'm praying that my Ray, to whom I was married for fifty-seven years, will look down from Heaven and be pleased with the poem about his little buddy.

To Our Special One Who's Sleeping Up Above

You are so sweet and oh so kind,
A better person I'll never find.
Life has a way of turning things around,
Still hearing your voice is a beautiful sound.
Through the years you suffered so,
How to help you I didn't know
Then I remembered how loving you are,
In my book you are my shining star.
When you said, *I can't even stand*,
Thank you for letting me hold your hand.
Through the pain you hung in there,
I didn't know how much more you could bear.
At the end you couldn't stand up straight,
All because the pain was so great.
We all didn't know what to do or say,
So the good Lord said, *Come My way*.
Now all who love you come together,
Just to let you know we love you forever.
This is not the end,
Just a little curve around the bend.

Albertine Self
Brooklyn, NY

Looking Pretty

Just for you my love I will look pretty.
I want you to gaze upon my beauty
    And remember me.
I want your vision of me to be pleasant.
I will laugh and smile
    Because for you I will look pretty.
Darling, I will look pretty because I want what
    You see on the outside of me to represent
    The beauty within me.
I want to be the paint covering your canvas,
    So for you I will look very pretty.

Bozana Belokosa
Pasadena, CA

Summer Nights by the Pool

The summer air without a care is still and warm.
The night is bright with the lights in the pool.
We swim like Olympians, until we are done in
And dripping with no sun to dry us, fire pit beside us.
We roast our hot dogs and toast our marshmallows.
Smoky and dry we rely on the juicy watermelon
That quenches our thirst; we think we'll burst.
Then we decide to swim again.
This time for pleasure and leisure, our backs on rafts
To see the crafts the stars design with us in mind.

Alison A. Robinson
West Hills, CA

You Are the One

You've lived 3/4 of your life, and you feel…
You've loved your best lover,
Kissed the best kisser,
Made love with the best.

Then, your true love comes along,
And all of what you thought
Goes right out the window.

When you meet the *one* who's able to
Take your breath away…
With just a look.

Someone who kisses so passionately,
And with each one of his touches,
You just melt into them.

Someone who loves your body—just the way it is.
Someone who makes love to your body—
So effortlessly, you go into another state of being.
It's magical, and all the pieces fit perfectly.

And all you can say is…
Hallelujah

Carol D. Brewer
Pomona, CA

I've been writing poetry for about forty years, mostly about love; I'm a hopeless romantic. We have to find the people we love, find the work we love, and the hobbies we love—which will make for a well-rounded life. I've recently taken up urban ballroom dancing classes and I love it. A thank you to my friend who continues to inspire me to write about love.

Spending Time with God

Have you ever played hooky?
Have you just disappeared?
Have you just let go for a while
And become one with God?
Have you lain on a blanket
And felt the warm sun
Watching the clouds go by?
God wrote stories in them
With answers to life —
To your many questions.
A mighty pirate ship races
For the pot of gold.
A small turtle looks ahead
Beating the foolish hare.
Maybe, God says slow down.
Don't fight with life!
Enjoy the world's beauty.
Listen to the bird's songs.
Experience a full life!
Send the dark gloom away.
Feel God's peace in you.
Don't run from your world.
Fill your world with *love*!
Spend time with God!
Answers will come soon.

Martha Weller
Mora, MO

You Are

You are the light of my life
I feel I know you since then,
forever.
Just by holding your hands
and gazing into your loving eyes
I see your soul undress in front of mine
trembling in my presence then and now
remembering that time, in the other life,
when we were lovers.
Now we embrace ourselves in this affair
so pure and sweet without carnal desires,
just an unadulterated friendship
in an eternal, loving way,
because *you are my friend*

Marcella White
Bronx, NY

An Old Man's Dream

I dreamed that we all lived in Heaven.
  It was beautiful.

I dreamed that we were told we would all go to Earth.
  "You'll all receive a physical body."

I dreamed that I asked, why?
  "There you can learn what you truly want."

I dreamed that I asked, why?
  "There you can learn who you truly are."

I dreamed that I asked, why?
  "There you can learn how to truly love."

I dreamed that I asked, why?
  "Everything else dies, only love truly lives forever."

I dreamed that I did not ask why.
  I truly want to learn how to love and live forever.

Loren D. Crane
Cave Creek, AZ

The Chestnut Tree

To gaze upon the chestnut tree;
to seek the wisdom of its leaves.
What have you heard? What have you seen
as the seasons turned from brown to green?
In the midst of fear you stood your ground
and watched the horror all around.
Many lives were torn apart
from the tired spirit to the young at heart.
Could you remember all of them?
The hundreds of thousands that passed your realm?
I don't know, but I am sure of two
grounded nearly the same as you.
Perhaps God put you there to pause
these children of the holocaust,
to give them hope instead of fear,
to say to them, *I'm always here*
to remind you of the world outside
and to keep your secret as you hide.
Years have passed and they are gone.
Yet you remain so tall and strong.
Still they hear you in the wind
as you echo again and again.
We are friends forever — you and me.
Forever yours, the chestnut tree.

Dea Floyd
Monroe, VA

My poem is about the chestnut tree outside of Anne Frank's secret
annex. It was written before the tree had to be cut down, but while it
was there it served as a very inspirational purpose of hope and joy.

Looking Back

I miss the extra money.
Not that I had a lot,
but when I worked and loved it
each day was full of thoughts
of maybe buying something
for the house or shop or me.
Or maybe planning traveling
to some place I'd like to see.
But now I have a lot of time
to think about the past
and the many times we traveled,
how I wish that it could last.
Things are very different now
with nothing much to do,
but try to fill each day
With *love* and pleasant memories, too.

La Rue Mumaw
Apollo, PA

Searching for a Treasure

Once upon a time, a long time ago
I sailed my ship on the pond, the wind did blow
I was a fearsome pirate, wooden sword in my hand
I ran as fast as I could, brought my ship to land
I searched for a treasure, buried it by a tree
Found a rock full of glass, it's a treasure to me
I marked the spot so I'll find it one day
And then I put my sailing ship away

I grew up, sailed a ship far across the sea
Searching for a treasure, where can it be
I wandered for years, sailed this world around
But what I'm looking for couldn't be found
I'm not quite sure what I'm looking for
But I think I'll know when I've found it
It'll be a wonderful thing I can't live without
Everyone will know, I'll probably yell and shout

And now at last I've finally come home
I put up the ship no more will I roam
There is the pond and there is the tree
The memories bring back the young boy in me
Now I know what I wanted was always here
The rock was just a symbol of all I held dear
Home is my treasure with all those I love
All the memories I've made is my treasure trove

Shirley A. Miller
Mountain Home, AR

Does It Have to Be This Way?

Have you not noticed how much things have changed?
No one seems to matter to anyone! I find that very strange.
You hear about a community that has suffered utter devastation,
but it seems there are few to bother the *why* to question!
What ever happened to the concept that we're to love our neighbor?
Has it become so *old fashioned* that you ignore that question?
It hurts my heart to hear about some of the things happening today.
Is that really what we're to expect from neighbors, day by day?
Surely we are smart enough to see what all the problems are.
If we change our attitude about the problems it will carry us far.
How can people sleep at night with hate simmering away inside?
Don't they want the peace they'd have by setting hate aside?
Surely the way things are now isn't the way it always has to be!
We have evolved enough, I feel, the consequences to see.
Wouldn't it be wonderful if every one of us stepped outside our door,
to get to know our neighbors, and learned to love once more?
No! It doesn't have to stay the devastating way it is right now.
We *all* are the same family and we will resolve it—somehow!

Sandy Cook
Rocklin, CA

I have been memorizing, reading and writing poetry since I was nine. I am now in my eighty-seventh year, and writing is what "helps me keep my sanity" (as one of my poems relates). I have a collection at this time of two hundred of the poems I have written in the last fifteen years. I've lost track of the ones before that. My only purpose in writing is to share, and I hope those reading my thoughts will be amazed or inspired!

Passin' Through

With all that's happening in our nation and world,
we all have fear.
This is the time for self-evaluation, and holding
the Lord ever so near.

When we feel lonely, worried, stressed and blue,
we need to stop, say a prayer, and remember
we are all just passin' through.

When all is said and done, and our bodies are becoming
weak — don't cry.
We need to remember that God is always with us,
He is by our side.

No matter what happens, what's important is how we
spiritually grew.
And when our last day comes, we'll know that we really
were just passin' through.

Marshelle Carberry
Fresno, CA

A Day at the Beach

Dusk is fast approaching, engulfing the ocean,
beach and boardwalk—the waves, in the diminishing
light constantly rolling, the ocean never stopping,
rising up white and crashing on the beach then
receding and starting the process again.
   Standing, waiting for the wind to pick up,
kite in one hand, string in the other, anxious to see
it flying high over crashing waves and sandy beach—
here comes the wind, kite up, up and away, more
string, stepping back and forth, side to side.
Arms straight up trying hard to keep it up, but
knowing the wind plays the main character here,
and has the upper hand in keeping the colorful kite
floating in the dwindling light. Over beach and ocean,
how lucky you are, Mr. Kite, to see such a beautiful sight.
   The boardwalk for the most part is deserted
now that night is upon us. Looking over at the ocean
you can see the white of the waves as they rise up in
the darkness. But in darkness or daylight you always
hear the constant motion of the ocean and the
crashing of waves upon the beach.
   Two lovers now hand in hand strolling the
boardwalk. The whole boardwalk is theirs, only an
occasional passerby. The bustling world has ceased
to exist, only miles of empty boards to see, no hurry,
no worry, complete contentment.

Anita Rogers
Royersford, PA

Saint Wycliffe of Miami

I pray that God's mercy and grace sustains us.
May our foes who try to hinder fail,
Jesus, please fulfil all our hopes, we pray.
All the tools of the devil we render powerless,
A mighty spiritual nuclear missile decimates him.
We have won our rights and freedom tactically.
Thank You, God, all our prayers have been answered.

Wycliffe Tyson
Miami Beach, FL

The Mustard Seed

Sift my soul, O Lord, that I might be worthy of Your will, being
pure enough in the colander of life to enter into Your Kingdom of
peace and joy. Inside the grains of life is like searching for a mustard
seed, hidden in a barrel of mixed-up seeds, the search goes on day
after day. The heart at times seems to reach further into the soul,
reaching then lost, till the next moment of love, the love that only
God can give, a beg of the soul to hold on to God's perfect love.
Happiness, contentment and joy to rise up and face another day.

Finally, giving up the seed and the search and finding within holds
all the world's mustard seeds and all God's love you can hold.

Marilyn Love
East Bernstadt, KY

My Journey of Life

The journey of my life has been long
My mom dreamed a tiger followed her home when I was born
My dad gave me to a Buddhist temple as a monk to save me
from death
War drove me from home and at 16 years old I joined the army
Two atomic bombs brought world peace
With the help of an American missionary, I accepted Jesus as
my Savior
God took me by a steamship across the Pacific Ocean to the
United States
He granted me advanced degrees, fellowships, and professorships
He helped me to be a writer, editor, columnist and a minister of
the Gospel
He put me in several international Who's Who record books
He is using me in evangelism by radio, TV, and on an Internet
Discipleship Institute
He arranged for me to be involved in the establishment of
several missions
His Word has been spread and His name is glorified
I thank Him for His grace and praise Him for His faithfulness
The journey of my life has been long
I am now ninety years old
I will do His will until I shall see my Father in Heaven.

Micah Leo
Vista, CA

*I was a soldier during World War II, a student of science, an editor of two
monthly magazines, a doctor of philosophy, a professor of chemistry, a fellow
of American Institute of Chemistry, a minister of the Gospel, the president
of a theological seminary, an author of several books, a columnist of two
newspapers, a winner of the poet's choice, a member of the International Poetry
Hall of Fame, the founder of Christ Society of Poets, and am presently the
editor-in-chief of the Psalms Today and the President of Christ Center Gospel
Mission. I am a sinner saved by Jesus Christ.*

Jace Declan

My son, my hope, my breath,
You are my sunrise and sunset.

I cry in joy and in sorrow because I had you…
and then lost you on the morrow.

I love you more than life's many travels…
Before I never knew what I was missing was you,
I thought life was grand, settled and fun,
and now I can't imagine how I ever felt like I was done.

The miracle of life is imagined in you,
and to that notion my miracle in life has come true.

My son, my reason, my gift from God,
I thank you for giving me strength that will never be gone.

I will protect, and love, and hold your hand.
I will teach, and reason, and help you understand.

My son, my hope, my breath from now on,
it is for you that I strive,
it is with you that I belong…

Justin J. Smith
Yakima, WA

Living in San Diego

Where the zonies trot
When it gets too hot!
Where the snowbirds fly
When snow is falling from the sky
Where aliens rob
When they want to steal a job
Where artists escape
To paint a seascape
Where convicts run
If they want to steal a gun
Where old folks retire
If they still have a desire
Where the sky is blue all day long
San Diego, I love you—forever in a song!

Marc B. Stein
San Diego, CA

Jesus as the Joy of One's Heart

Jesus wants to be the joy of your heart.
there is nothing like the joy of His love.
Keep Jesus as the joy of your heart,
for you will find more love, peace, and
joy in your life, like no other.

It also spills over to people around you.
Bring that joy into what you do, and
share it with others around you, and
watch the joy bring a smile upon that
person.

Jesus is the master of that joy, and
is always the true faithful one in
grace, and peace through His Salvation
for us, in which he gave all upon the
cross.

No matter how far you fall from
His grace, He will always pick you
up and love you in the joy and
peace of His salvation for us.

Lord, thank You for the joy
and love from Your heart.

Carol A. Miller
Washingtonville, NY

Grandma's Zinnias, Pekingese, and Rhubarb Pies

Grandma wears straw hat,
at edge of sidewalk in breeze,
next to her Zinnias,
swaying happily in sun,
smiling at her Pekingese.
Her farmhouse stood proud,
birds, butterflies, bees play,
under shady elms,
Grandma jokes with Jim and I,
we drink spring water from the pump.
Rhubarb has grown thick,
patches near garage, driveway,
promise of a pie,
rabbits, squirrels, crickets glad,
in cool grass, wildflowers.
Grandpa mows, picks corn,
Grandma, Jim, and I work, too,
weed, water Zinnias,
feed Pekingese, pick Rhubarb,
which we all knew she loved.

William D. Irwin
Princeton, IL

My brother Jim and I want to thank our dear Grandma Palmer for helping us, motivating us, and inspiring us all of our lives (from little kids into adulthood), to make something good, positive, and constructive with our lives and to be the best people we can be (dedicated, vital and contributing members of our communities and society), as we (with God's love and grace), share our gifts, talents and aptitudes with our families, friends, and everyone.

Wisdom

I write these words not just for you and me
I write these words for the world to see
Who let Lucifer through the gate
To fill the world with all his hate?
Now our world is so full of unrest
Before us we are given our biggest test
To unite together and do our best
To have world peace is God's plan
Together to make it happen in this beautiful land
Just reach out, touch, and hold a hand
For remember who gave us this promised land
Now people live love and make your stand

Agatha Broza
Lansing, IL

Life

Life is an ember —
the glowing remains
  of life
Through pain and grief
  and strife.
Breath is its keeper —
a guardian of the soul
  that heals in sleep.
The heart is a boundary —
the gate that will swing wide
  and welcome you inside.
Life to share is all there is.
It need not always be the
  best to shine,
even in the worst times,
a door with no key,
a mist through which you
  could not see.

Connie R. Holt
Waynesboro, TN

Our New Treasure

We have a new treasure,
A treasure that's loved beyond all measure.
Yes, it's a baby boy! And have you guessed?
He's established himself as our pride and joy!

There's a bright, winning twinkle in his eye.
There's a sly boyish grin that's being given a try.
There's a cute little nose, a proud little chin.
There are fingers and toes each adding up to ten.

Yes, he's perfect! And here we might mention,
Although being a big sister is a trifle bit new,
Ellie Blu knows Grayson Taylor
Has made *our treasures* two!

Florence C. Tibbs
Las Vegas, NV

Ariana

She came into my life
On a hot August day,
One of God's greatest gifts,
Perfect in every way.

I now claimed a new title —
Not just daughter, wife, mother.
Thanks to God for blessing me.
I was now a grandmother.

Barbies, puppy dogs, and bubblegum
Have all been traded in.
Now it's clothes, music, proms,
And texting her best friends.

Her beautiful smile
And sweet, gentle ways
Can bring sunshine
Into the darkest days.

May her guardian angel take over
When my time on Earth has passed.
May her memories of me
Throughout her lifetime last.

Carolyn Fuller
Anna, IL

A Reason for Everything

Life is not a showcase.
There's a reason for everything.

The rhythm of autumn knows its flowers and forests.
The powerful wind is familiar with profound winters.
The woodman is unaware of the murmuring of trees he chops.
And of ones whose wood end in musical sounds
Everything has a reason…

Surrounding wind swarms the emerald sea moving wooden ships
as the tranquil moon breaks through a brush of dark clouds.
Everything has a reason.

Even in our tormented world, the night sky sings as it presents us
with lavishing perfumed scents from blooming trees.
Everything has a reason…

To maintain hope in our hearts from a shooting star.
For we are replicas of bright stars which encourage us to gain
peace and calm.
We can learn to appreciate our neighbors and our world.
We can only achieve complacency by good deeds and not by
indifference.
Spiritual perfection makes the difference in our hearts…

And the reason for everything.

Frances N. Contreras
Clearwater, FL

My most joyful memories of childhood were spent in the beautiful island of Puerto Rico where I was born. My life has been a mix of tragic and happy events. I never gave up hope. I cherish New York City where I received education and the opportunity to become an elementary school educator. I'm now retired in Florida and sing in a choir. I'm grateful for the release of emotion in writing poetry. Poetry is my passion. Also, for all the blessings bestowed upon me. I dedicate this poem to my children and grandchildren with love.

My Dad's Connection Throughout Time

Last night, in one of my many dreams
My dad visited me... like many times before
He's always smiling, and looks the same
As he did in 1963. He passed away much too young
At the age of 53.

He was the greatest influence in my life
A man of very few words
Yet, I knew he was always there
Sometimes in my most troublesome days
He still shows me the way.

I know within my innermost self
My problems are really opportunities... in disguise
I should treat them all as such
In actuality... they all really
Don't amount to much
In the *big picture*.

In my dream last night... I was traveling on a train
Sitting alone... and happy
When Dad walked by and said
"Hi babe, how are you? We haven't talked for a while."
I couldn't have been happier
Just to see his smile.

Waking up this morning... early
Getting ready for my day
I knew I had another glimpse of heaven
Knowing it's not far away.

Jó Ann Boggs Cordova
Hesperia, CA

*This poem was written March 22, 2015 on my parents' wedding anniversary.
They married in 1931, and I was born in 1932. My mother Mildred passed
away in 2002. Being an only child, I was always a Daddy's girl from my first
recollection. My parents are both still very strong in the spirit world. She and
my dad were a hard act to follow, because of the stability in their marriage. I
wanted the same white picket fence that I had as a child. Today, with a lot of
twists and turns, I have that life through their teachings.*

Jehovah God Cares

Wherever you go,
Whatever you do,
Always trust in Jehovah.
He will see you through.
You cannot see Him,
but He is always there.
You are never far
from His loving care.
He created the earth
and placed it in space.
Then He created
the human race.
He is our father
and protects us each day.
He guides us through life
as we work and play.
When we are troubled or in need of help,
we can go to Him in prayer.
He will comfort and help you
with the greatest of care.

Mary Alice Seiter
Lexington, MI

Windows

God gives
light when it's dark
sun to warm us when we are cold
cool breeze when we are warm
strength when we are weak.
Encouragement for our soul
short or tall. Big or small,
meets all our needs
when we call.
Picks us up when we fall.
All these blessings even
more we cannot receive
through the windows of
Heaven. He sends His love.
He does it all.
Mal 3: KJV

Gladys R. Witt
Hamersville, OH

Faded Bullets

Many a night young men and women
  Dream of becoming soldiers.
They want to fight for our country
  And for what they believe.

Too many Americans
  Have sat and watched
Faded bullets
  Falling from the sky.

Our precious soldiers
  Want to win the victory seat
By dodging the bullets at an
  Unmarked scene.

Some will come home
  And tell their families
Of how exciting
  Their combat was.

While others will not make it
  As they witness
A magnificent scene of dancing bullets
  In the sky.

Sherie P. Parks
Cedar City, UT

Ache No More

Oh, be still my bleeding heart.
Why do you ache so?
Is it because of loved ones passed?
Is it because your mother and father
are up in Heaven
doing the work of the Lord?
Or do you ache for all the people
of the world gone bad?

Too much of the world gone,
too much death.
Oh, be still my bleeding heart.
God has a plan for those people
gone wrong.
Oh, be still my bleeding heart.
God is here to help you
ache no more.
So be still, and ache no more.

Dianne Hill
Morris, IL

Something different for you all. With all the bad stuff going on in the world, I am just trying to put smiles on the world. Even if it is for just a little while, we all need to smile. Our loved ones would want us to smile. Pray for those who have lost for no reason. Pray for peace.

Flowers Given in Different Ways

Flowers can be given or spoken
We can see them or hear kind words
The ones in the vase we can smell
The verbal flowers time did tell

One can hold them or hear them
They are both flowers in different ways
The ones in the vase will sadly fade away
The spoken flowers happily will always stay

The spoken flowers given
Were words he had listened
Of things you said one day
He returned it as a compliment in another way
Which led to this kind of flower
That you could hear and give you a tear.

Therese Jacques Gamache
Chepachet, RI

This poem came about when I received a compliment from a friend. I thought she just gave me some flowers — the ones you feel but don't see.

Music the Healer

I've danced with black beauties,
I've danced with British beauties,
I've danced with all kinds of cuties
In my youth.

But none can compare with my lovely
  wife Ethel,
And that is the truth.
But the point I wish to make,
For God's sake,
Is that music is the healer.
North and South,
East and West,
Music is the best.

In these hot summer days,
As music plays,
Barry wrote the songs,
And wrote no wrongs,
The Boss is of course
A great songwriter,
But none can compare
With music out there.

Alfred Elkins
Bronx, NY

The Milky Way's Hymn of Praise

My thick clustered bands
Paint the heavn's like a flood,
There silently shouting
The glory of God!
Splashed across the vast ether
Like a diamond of light,
Reflecting His radiance
Through the wonders of night.
He spoke me to being,
I pulsed with His flame,
I danced to His brightness
To praise His great name!
And though you might marvel
That I illumine the sky,
I sing the awed praises
Of One greater than I.
I show forth His splendor,
His marvelous ways,
As I silently sing Him
My anthem of praise.

Joyce Keedy
Towson, MD

Creation sparkles with God's glory and eternally sings His praise! I rejoice to worship my matchless Lord and Savior Jesus and join this glorious symphony to praise Him. I was born July 23, 1957. I love teaching music lessons; to date I have taught over eight hundred children and adults to play musical instruments. I was the organist of Presbyterian Church 1981–2010 and organist of Calvary Baptist since early 2016. My favorite places are the ocean, my flower garden, and caverns. I had the great privilege of playing Luray Caverns' famous stalactite organ in 1994. I have published six poetry books, and my seventh, Celebrate His Praise, *will be published this year.*

Play's End

Life is like a play with no author
Jolts, surprises:
All jostling on the trail of time
As strange shapes in a vision:
Mundane curtain of day, night
Discloses
Play's end: exit to a real world of light.

L. J. London
Shaker Heights, OH

In My Neighborhood

Cottonwood seedlings
arrive along with fish flies,
Soon gone with the breeze.

Standing in sunshine,
rain is falling on my head.
I see a rainbow.

Hall of fame for cops.
Hall of shame for murderers.
Lord knows who goes where.

Constance Warren
Detroit, MI

Empty Places in the Pew

In years gone by, when singing at church, I used to look out and see
Old and dear friends of many years, who meant a lot to me.
They sat there every Sunday in the same place in the pews
Smiling up when they saw me as I sat within their view.

It seems like only yesterday that these old friends were there.
Life was good, their smiles were sweet, and there was love to share.
But then life changed so subtly and they began to slip away
To that very special blessed place where I hope to see them
 again someday.

These friends had helped to shape my life for all those many years.
They had seen me through the good times, the bad times, and
 the tears.
Their love had been the anchor I needed in the storm.
When my life was tossed and hope was gone, they kept me safe
 from harm.
They had been the stalwart helpmates who helped to make me see
That no matter what obstacles I encountered they were always
 there for me.

But now when I return to church and look out at the pews
Of the friends who used to be there, now there are very few.
I grieve because they aren't where they used to be, and we are
 far apart.
But I know deep down inside me, they're with me safe within
 my heart.

Margaret Hauber
Grandview, MO

A Word of Wisdom

History beckons wisdom's knowledge urging American
Voters to restore the nation's foundational views, which
Were based on virtue, ethics, and freedom of faith.

History gave the nation a plan to live free in peace,
To worship God, or not, as you wish, and to pursue
Happiness with ease.

History gave the nation a government to ensure fair
Treatment for all, giving respectful dignity to even
Those who fail and fall. History looked to the future
With trust toward tomorrow's leaders to safeguard the
Nation's democracy for all who live in its light.

When history is *now* we choose a new leader (with
Trust in our hearts) who will guard America, the
Lighthouse of hope and democracy.

Don't let distractions or lies make you confused; just
Vote for the principles that identify you. Look beyond
The candidates to the philosophical values they represent.
If the values are not yours then step aside; say to
Yourself, *This just isn't me. I cannot abide.* Say,
Adieu and take your vote to the other side where
you and your values reside. Stand tall and proud as you
Make your mark for American views that stand for you.

Mable M. Guiney
Ft. Walton Beach, FL

*I have loved history ever since my second grade teacher Mrs. Fields began
each school day with the Pledge of Allegiance to America's flag. This was
followed by the class singing "My Country 'Tis of Thee" and then "The West
Virginia Hills." This daily routine in the East Williamson Elementary
School (Mingo County, WV) set a firm foundation for students to become
American patriots with respect for the flag and a love for West Virginia's
beautiful hills. Our schools today need firm instructional routines for each
day's class in order to cultivate good citizenship.*

Why?

Imagine a little girl
A tear in her eye
She dreams by her window at night
A whisper of wonder and pretend
Always hoping that her sorrow would end

She wants to be free to fly with the angels
Or run and play in her magic garden
Or jump in the ocean and swim with the dolphins
Always wishing she was happy

I ask God, *why?*

Carl A. Weaver
Glenview, IL

Mute Love

I love you my, darling Amber, deeply,
though with my tongue and lips I cannot sing or speak.
My feelings for you are bold and strong,
not frail or meek.

Though I must express my feelings for you with my hands,
or words on a printed page.
I love you deeply on a grand scale,
a scale I cannot gauge;

when I am near you, my soul burns with a searing flame
and my heart beats and pounds.
All this within my mortal frame,
though where silence has lease, love really abounds.

When we are alone I like to touch your pretty face.
I like to run my fingers through your soft, downy hair.
Though I am calm and cool in my mind,
you make my emotions erupt volcanically and flair.

I dream of taking walks with you on warm summer days
alone and peaceful in our own private realm.
We can frolic in a lake or have picnics
sitting in the shade of a good sturdy elm.

Realistically, of course, we can't spend all our time together
  holding hands kissing and wishing.
We have to go about our daily duties, which often keeps us alone,
  separated and apart.
But I want you to understand, my dear Amber, and believe this:
Though I spend my days in silence, no man can have as much love
  for you as the amount of love deep within my heart.

Alan Knight
Champaign, IL

Love

Love is a word some people might say
But it's really our action what we do every day
Love brings pleasure by touch or smile
To make someone happy, or just visit awhile

Love is so much more than we understand
It goes beyond all reason and power of man
You cannot drown it with water or burn it with fire
It lives on forever and never grows tired

Love is one thing you can have every day
No power on Earth can take it away
Money can't buy it; it must be free
It is a gift from God, to you and to me

Many go through life and never really know
How much they are loved in this world below
Maybe there's someone in your life today
Who needs you to say, *I love you*

Helon Phillips
Cordesville, SC

A *Got-for* Moment

Circled round the table for the third time,
I am beginning to think I have totally lost my mind.
Now what did I come out into the kitchen for?
Was I headed to go out the back door?
Was I going to the sink to get a drink?
I know the garden needs weeded and has to be done.
There are clean dishes that need to be taken care of
And wet clothes that need hung.
There was a good reason coming out here—what was it for?
I have not a clue; my thinking has become very poor.
My mind's in turmoil, my thoughts are in a constant boil.
At least I'm not alone; I can get the dog a bone!
The more I try to recall what was important on my mind,
My list grows longer, and a reason I can't find.
When my son was young, I would ask him why he did
The little silly things he did.
He'd shrug his little shoulders and tell me,
"I got for, Mom!" He was such an intelligent kid.
Instead of saying, I forgot! It came out jumbled.
I am not getting older; my mind has just stumbled.
I have not lost my mind; I have a *got-for* moment!
I'll take the lesson from when my son
Was so very young and so much fun.
So, to heck with trying to figure it out!
I will just get a glass of milk to drink
And have myself a cinnamon bun!

Clio H. Gerbes
Canisteo, NY

Twenty Little Angels

Babies are a miracle
We know this to be true
God gives us these angels
To love and care for, too
Every day they're growing
And soon they are off to school
Making friends and playing
And learning the golden rule

One dark and senseless moment
A young man with a heart of stone
Made his way to school that day
Shot and killed everyone in the room
Twenty little children lost their lives that day
And there were six heroes
Who died being ever so brave

The world cried out in sorrow
This never should have been
But we know that these angels
Are in Heaven with golden wings
We must all remember
To thank the Lord above
For having known these babies
Who are angels on Earth to love

Sophia Thompkins
Tolland, CT

USA — Today

I'm just an old woman
Cleaning around town,
Trying not to allow
Our new laws to bring me down.

The same-sex marriage,
We can't pray aloud,
Or even fly a flag
Of which some were once proud.

Every new law they pass
Throughout God's land
Is defying His word,
Giving Satan the upper hand.

So I may go to jail
When there's no Pledge of Allegiance,
No freedom of speech,
And His word we can't preach.

Mary Hamner
Kahoka, MO

Recalling My Mother

When Mother's Day comes
I recall my own mother
Who paid the debt of nature
In my absence

I was living far away from my mother
Exactly a half circle of the earth
When she passed away
I was seriously ill

Unable to bid farewell to my virtuous mother
Who would be interred in the churchyard
My heart was suddenly pained day and night
As if pierced by a sharp knife

I felt pity for my mother
Who was utterly miserable throughout her life
To raise her young children
Who became fatherless at an early age

I entreated my dead-mother's soul earnestly
To forgive my deficiency towards her
For I was an ungrateful child
Who has since repented throughout his life…

Minh-Vien Nguyen
San Francisco, CA

Teresa—In Memory Of

When first we met,
you reminded me so much
of your mother.

Each time we got together,
I felt your mom's presence
so close to me again.

I thank you for those moments
and wish you well as you
cross over to the Spirit World.

Your Mom, Ava, Sandy,
Brenda and Joel will be so
happy to have you with
them in Paradise.

Guy B. Young
Grants Pass, OR

Faithful Jesus

I will never, never leave you
I always will be there
I never will forsake you
You are always in My care

Tho' mountains fall into the sea
And earthquakes cause distress
Makes no difference, I am there
You always will be blessed

My word is true, it cannot fail
I'm ever by your side
I made a covenant with you
And I am God, I cannot lie

The storms will come
The seas will roar
And trials press you sore
But just remember, I am there
And I will see you through

I promised to be with you
Until the very end
So be at peace and walk in love
I am your faithful friend

Doris Applegate
Harlan, IN

My life has been a testimony of the above poem. At eighty-five years old, God has proven to be a true and faithful friend! Because of our fear now of terrorism and other traumas going on, I felt this poem would be an encouragement to all who read it!

Making My Way Through Dementia

Armand, my husband, has dementia.
How do I deal with this disease?
Each day something new happened
Oh, Lord, I need your help, please.

I had to realize this wasn't his fault
Because I didn't know anything at all
To help me control my anger and such,
For his memory was getting small.

There are classes to attend once a month
To learn how others deal in their life.
Dementia is very confusing, demanding, etc.,
Including bits and pieces of strife.

I keep my husband active in helping me
In feeding the birds, doing dishes, or whatever.
I tell him that we will get through this each day
With the Lord's help; we need to work together.

All My Love,
Your Wife, Gloria

Gloria M. Bouley
Plainfield, CT

My husband is ninety-seven years young and a World War II veteran. My husband is a great inspiration to me. He was diagnosed with dementia in January 2016. I will always love him forever. I began writing poetry in the mid-sixties. In 1996, I created my own personal greeting cards. My poems are stories in my life. When I can, I still write poetry. I enjoy wildlife, photography, and knitting. I thank the Lord for each day. I take it one day at a time and live it to the fullest.

Soul Possessions

Objects of my desires found in the heart
Rhythms of emotions that make you dance
When you cannot explain what you feel
The soul possessions of your inner self
Glowing happiness like when the moon shines
So bright as with the stars in the sky
Being on top of the world and free falling
Soaring through life with joy and laughter
Just letting go and setting sail
Expressions of satisfaction and accomplishment
When your dreams have become a reality
How your feelings are never justified words
These are just the possessions of the soul

Tyrone Glessner
Sacramento, CA

Who I Am

Look at me and you will see
a girl with brown hair and eyes,
wrinkles that prove I have experienced life,
but is that really me?
Did you know that when you see me
most likely I will be saying the rosary?
When I look back at you, I see
God's child whom I love;
you most likely become part of that rosary.
Know that when I feel a breeze on my face
I close my eyes, outstretch my arms
and thank God I've experienced this place.
I am a speck of dust that travels in life,
blows in the wind, and sees beauty within.
At the end please remember that I did exist.

Dolores Kutzer
Kill Devil Hills, PA

My Continuing Battle with Ants

I was standing by my kitchen counter the other day when I
noticed a scout ant coming my way.
When he saw a crumb that I had not wiped away he started
jumping up and down and shouting to the others.
Hey, fellas, look what I found, come gather around and let's
play zig-zag as we try to avoid the lady with the dish rag.
She may wipe away a bunch of us, but when she leaves
another crumb, those that are left will be here for lunch.
Then the game of zig-zag begins all over again.
Some will lose and some will win.
We outnumber her by thousands we were here before her
and we will be here long after she is gone.
There will always be another crumb to bring us
into another home.

Velma Anderson
Verbena, AL

Something to Ponder

Escape to a wonderful vacation
Get rest from a bad relation
Do anything your mind creates
All you need to procure this is
   Meditate

A quiet place only you can enter
In no time it will be your center
Such a small thing can have great power
To relieve life's stress in five minutes or an hour

By digging deep you can master
A sure way to make things go faster
A whimsical venture of your creation
Just pick your own time to relate and
   Meditate

Nona Reedinger
Tower City, PA

Grabber Hill

Tonight I'll walk Mary up Grabber Hill
In the light of the moon while everything's still.

I'll long for a kiss like so often I've done.
Oh, Lord, what a price to be in love with a nun.

I know she loves me, for I can see it in her eyes,
But all I get is a handshake and a goodbye.

I'll long for a kiss like so often I've done.
Oh, Lord, what a price to be in love with a nun.

When we get to Heaven, and I know we will,
I'll be with my Mary from Grabber Hill.

I know she will love me by the look in her eyes,
And there will be no more handshakes and no goodbyes.
I won't beg for a kiss like so often I've done.
Oh, Lord, what a price to be in love with a nun.

Etta L. Bailey
Loudonville, OH

Wanderer of the Road

Wanderer of the road,
That is what I'm called.
One day here, the other there,
Always on the walk.

On the dusty road I walk,
With my banjo on my arm,
No one else to talk to;
My best friend long has gone.

My feet are sore and tired
And my throat is dry, too.
The sun burns down like fire
And no shade to comfort you.

When I walked along the road
Then my eyes grew wide;
A wooden cross with words inscribed
Stood there along the side.

I sat down beside the cross
And took the banjo in my hands.
The song I played on him now,
My friend always liked the best.

The flowers that I picked
I laid beneath the cross;
Rest in peace here my friend
A wanderer of the road had lost.

Maria Vanderleek
Inverness, FL

Monja

My sunshine, remember, we came together in this far country.
We held hands and run to the magnificent ocean shore…
We laughed so loud that tears filled our eyes…
We talked and played in a language that does not exist.
We danced many nights in Key West to the rhythm of blues…
We artists found friendship, where my young soul met the old
  soul of yours
Often I ask myself:
As a painter, how can I paint the beauty, tenderness, caringness
  of you?
As a writer, how can I describe the sound of the universe
That you as a virtuoso compose on your piano?
As your mother, I tell myself, how happy I am
To see you in joy, to hear the sound of your voice
To smell your freshly washed hair
To know you give and receive kindness to friends
And love to your partner.
To recognize that you have become a beautiful woman,
Gifted with talent and honesty with endless love.
You are our pride, mine and your father's.
No words exist to tell you how much we love you…
May shining stars fulfill all your years to come…
Your happiness shall always grow, like trees…
And you stay healthy and fulfilled like the colors of spring
Always new.

Vesna Hanhart
Las Vegas, NV

*I write this poem for all women who would give their own life for their child.
In my first marriage, my firstborn children, twin boys, died. I got divorced
and went to study at the university to forget my pain. Ten years later, New
Year's Eve, I wished so much to have my child. Later in September, my daughter
Monja was born. No happier moment exists in my life! To me no nicer person
exists like she has become.*

Betrayal of the Heart

I have betrayed you, my love.
Lying beside you and pressing
your hand so tight against my chest,
my heart still yearns for the
sight of another.
I have betrayed you, my love.
I sigh so deep and my tears
roll down my cheeks for my
mind will not let go.
I have betrayed you, my love.
I have been unfaithful. You must
hurt, but jealousy is not right.
For he, who I named grief, is much
stronger than we.

Frances Saiz
Santa Fe, NM

Grief is an illness for those who just can't let go!

Keeping Glory

Do not let doom on parade dismantle glory
from every chapter writing on your story.
That shady march will help and sometimes will not
defines revolving case people living no doubt.
Here is where you cheer or have much less to shout.

The chapter that parades in your life today
could be changing epic brightness to mirror clay.
Still, always looking for the better summary
could lighten up blue episode some may run from.
You bless the next theme foretells right outcome.

Do not let doom on parade dismantle glory
from every chapter writing on your story.
Some choice theme more adept at beaming the light.
Most you will find it limits the entitlement.
But do not let the real glory soon out of sight.

Annette Stovall
San Fernando, CA

I have been writing poems for a while and am always eager to include my poem in Eber & Wein's Best Poets anthology. I was inspired to write this poem because of the problems we face in life. It is hoped this poem will offer some enlightenment.

The Winds of Change

We live, we laugh, we love
  What more can it be?

This life that was so carefree
Until it is taken away… suddenly!
  Since the atrocity of 9/11,
The winds have changed so dramatically!

For it had pitted one's life against another,
To bring the country from unity
  To later disunity.
When darkness fills one's soul
From the dangers that surrounds… *us*.

But are we to put blinders on or
  Look through those Rose-colored glasses,
  When hate fills the forces around… *us*.
  For those innocents who had their *blood shed*
  Will cry out for a new life!

Dorothy Safko
Harrisburg, PA

Not Too Late

It's not too late to tell them you love them
While you're alive and can talk, take the time
Forgive those who have wronged you, it's not too late
Pick yourself up from the mud and the hate
Dust everything off, walk with Jesus, heads high
Sing praises, shout victory, hands to sky, tears dry
Take time to enjoy your own life, relax and play
Games, travel, visit church sites along the way
Meet new, uplifting, positive, non-griping people
Those that plan forward willing to climb that hill
It's a relief coming from work or far places
To find everyone happily occupied with their graces
Not too late to find the matching mate
For those who would share their time and state
And pass and exceed obstacles or stumbling blocks
Not too late to discover what unlocks
Life's secrets which are not so secret
They're there in reality in front of us yet
To be garnered, latched upon, usurped
Using your mind's eye or seat of thought, intellect
Find yourself not too late to discern right from wrong
Drop what's bad, learn music and write a new song
Lovingly diligently each step in front of the other
No looking back but forward begin again forever
Freedom means freedom from mischief swords
NTL run toward Heaven's rewards

Joan Mays
West Brooklyn, IL

Thank you for including my work in your publication. Some of my work is inspired by the scriptures where it encourages people to write new material concerning words and works of the way to Heaven utilizing the Ten Commandments. Observing our mother and father cats meticulously caring for their kittens gives great insight to the other side of nature and the communications removed from humans in Genesis. Other works are "Cinder Road," "Adventures of Janie," and "Rock Your Way to Heaven." Our family associates with continuing education at the local community colleges.

All God's Children Bleed Red

In a world of trepidation where cowards spew hatred
and instill fear,
Let us stand together, our differences revered.
God's children all around the globe,
I call you my brothers and sisters,
A cloak of love to enrobe.

World leaders may blur the lines,
Pontificating our welfare, while shadowing solidarity
by benign or malign.
We all are connected, yet subjected to the
propaganda that divides our lives.
Tune out the noise, honor our differences, and rejoice.
Adherent in spirit, inherent as one.

Joy in birth, or grief in death, does not limit itself
to one race or creed.
Neither pain nor suffering knows any color, culture, or breed.
Compassion, empathy, does not one country or person own.
All humanity possess sentiments within our mortal
flesh and bones.
More similarities than differences define… humankind.

Lay down weapons and bandage hearts instead.
Cease the bloodshed.
For all God's children bleed red.

Leesa M. Garland
Nashville, TN

My hope is the meaning behind my poem is self-evident. Turn on the news and listen to the many tragedies all around the globe, affecting virtually every country, every race and creed. Victims, including innocent children, are caught in the crossfire of needless shootings or bombings. It not only saddens me, but sickens me. We derive from one creator; we are all connected, related in spirit and emotion. Please pray to end the senseless bloodshed of brothers and sisters everywhere.

The Garden

Your life resembled a velvet rose.
Each petal reached out in kindness to
    others, bringing smiles and peace.

We watched as you tenderly pruned and cared
    for the individual flowers.
Oh, the sweet fragrance of your personality
    touched many hearts.... Then you were gone.

Lying in your favorite place among the roses,
    surrounded by the soil in which they grew...

If only we knew.

Patty A. Burdette
North Port, FL

The Fawn

A softness lay
In new-cured hay
Touched by the warm June sun,
The reddish tawny spotted soft
Of a newborn fawn.
The windrow in which he lay
Protected the tiny life so new
From whatever harm came near.
As he rested beneath sky of blue,
The softness made not a sound,
Nor any movement did it show.
The little life lay as instructed
By mother who fed in field below.
As I gazed upon this softness,
It brought a touch of warm tenderness
To my heart.
I sent in silent prayer a plea
That a long life comes from this
Pure and precious start.

Catherine Smith
Bumpass, VA

Mirror, Mirror

Sun streaming through the window's curtain of lace
Flickering like fingers of fire upon my tortured face
The mirror knows me, sees my layers of anger
Funhouse mirrors where there is always danger
Who are you? You look lost and broken
Is that ribbon in your hair supposed to be a token?
Who did this to you, bound you in chains of shame?
Name it, fight it, shed your shroud of blame
You see a mere reflection it makes no choice
Dig beneath the bones and skin it's time to use your voice
Challenge yourself to love as often as petals fall
Seek love, life with grace beyond your carefully crafted wall
Look in the mirror and use the truth to change your course
You are the compass; change your direction, no fear, full force

Kay Jo Collins
Modesto, CA

The End of the Song

Music playing across an infinite constellation
Notes timely and melodious
The sounds ripple endlessly through to the stars
Reflecting destiny's patterns in formation

There are no frivolous births
No un-mourned deaths
Each man, woman, child, baby, and the unborn
Their love, potential, are of immeasurable worth

We shouldn't measure by talent or money
But a fragile heart that loves
Their inner music touches everything
Covering it with celestial honey

God created us all with a plan
How outrageous it must seem
When the music is violently torn from the stand
From the unborn child to the old black man

The heart stops, the instruments can't play or sing
Only then do we comprehend
The unending consequence, the silent void
The end of their song; our everything

Marcy L. Bowser
Newark, OH

An Endless Flight of Geese

The dogs and I ride down to the road on the scooter to collect
the mail.
I am stopped halfway there by overhead honking,
an endless line from horizon to horizon.
I stop counting at fourteen flocks. Hundreds wing by.
They bring such joy in their passing.
I have seen them in flocks like this twice lately.
I think the early spring like weather has made them more active.
Their shadows cover me, so dense a winged cloud they make.
Now day after day they continue to fly overhead.
The most I have ever seen here, a migration of living
feathered hearts.
The winged nation of brother beings.

Joan Hunt
Lebanon, OR

Incredible

Amazing your love stays
To remember and the total years of
62 are with me.
Thank you
For being you, Dad.
Your memories
Can't ever be *forgotten*,
Even when you've passed on and away to
Your next wonderful *new life*!
Love you, *Dad* —
Your daughter,
Cynthia

Cynthia M. Rose-Baratta
Jericho, NY

Papa's There

In hills of flint, hickory's yellow with
   scarlet oaks and black gum's crimson —
   Papa's there.
In rich mountain valleys, black and deep,
   wild strawberries, blackberry, meadowlark —
   Papa's there.
In wood smoke dying with the evening
   wind, smell of country ham, cackle of hen —
   Papa's there.
In sounds of daybreak, frosty cold, wood fire growing,
   owl's last call, rooster's hello —
   Papa's there.
In timber-cleared fields, broken to plow, whistle
   of quail, clank of milk pail —
   Papa's there.
In distant call of hunting hound, hunting horn,
   axe's ring, calves born —
   Papa's there.
In the smell of smokehouse and sugar-cured hams,
   hickory chips, walnuts on the ground —
   Papa's there.
In summer's heat, springhouse trips, dark water,
   cold buttermilk, waterdogs —
   Papa's there.
In boyhood hunts, for man and boy, squirrels
   (the excuse of being together),
    huckleberries as fare —
   Papa's there.
In trees and plants named and shown, shame weed,
   watercress, limestone fern, time to give, love to share —
   Papa's there.
In love's perfect place, a soul's retreat, life's quest,
   rest, memory —
   Papa's there.

Carl B. Reed
Altus, OK

Where the Red Fern Grows *is like my story as a boy. The movie is about the same area.*

Why I Write

I like to write short lines that rhyme
They don't come easy but it kills time
To write what I think and use my head
Hoping it's good enough to bring in the bread

I'll never be another Poe
He wrote sad tales, too sad for my dough
I like to leave my readers with a grin
Better than some macabre sin

People who read poetry are above the lot
Good poetry will always hit a tender spot
I write my lines so I can grow
It's not for love it's for the dough

Edward Cohen
Glen Oaks, NY

Amazing Grace and Tuff Love

Amazing grace and tuff love
a rare combination
in this world
those whose innocence is lost
can't be blamed
suffer secretly, silently
through their pent-up pain
can reclaim
their innocence and walk
without guilt or shame
Be the child
who leads us
Make America grateful again
unto the Lord

Roy A. Smith
West Columbia, SC

Wedding

With each new passing day,
Time is rapidly slipping away.
Many notes have been made.
Many plans we had to trade.

Dresses are of white and blue,
Bouquets, hair, and nails left to do.
Parties are all planned and in place.
Oh yes, we can't forget the wedding cake.

This special day holds joy and tears.
Put aside all your doubts and fears.
Man and woman become as one.
God's great plan is completely done.

Erma L. Stephens
Van Wert, OH

And No One Cares That No One Cares

How I marvel as time goes by
Of dazzling sunsets in blazing skies
Of thunderclouds in angry shades
Of rusted sighs
Bright yellows open up my eyes
Rainbows hued to hypnotize
Every day a different scheme
Everyone a different dream
Yesterday, fluffy clouds costumed in angry shades of
White, black, and grey
Danced to the rhythms the thunder bolts play
Exotic zigling of multi-colored shapes as unique as
Each day
A multi-colored arched handkerchief wiped the eyes
Of the darkened heavens' humble skies
After great gulps of countless tears
Had covered this universe of countless years
Spectacular, phenomenal, lovingly given shares
And no one cares that no one cares.

Sharon D. Proehl
Henderson, NV

Will It Ever Be?

I wanna be the one with you,
needing to know if this love is something I never knew.
Trying to see my life as a journey through heartache and love,
without thinking I can trust my heart too much.
I want to feel the feeling that others feel in their hearts,
wanting to know a love that will never fall apart.
All I can do is try and love with all my heart's content;
the hardest part is finding someone to fall in love with.
I go through days wondering where I can find the love,
never knowing if my heart will ever be good enough.
I think of reasons why I can't always move on,
believing that my love felt so strong.
Always wanting to tell someone how I truly feel
is not easy when love doesn't always feel like it's real.
You're the one that makes me feel like I belong,
never leaving my side or ever letting me down.
I have tried to forget, but it's just too hard to bear,
the pain, the sadness, and the memories we share.
Will I ever be the one who ends the hurt and pain,
to be forever with certainty of loving again?
I need to be the one with you always,
in heart, feelings, or some words to say.
If you feel that your heart needs time to think,
just be honest to my heart: will it ever be?

Kolten C. Koeppen
Jolley, IA

Nobody Knows

Nobody knows the person inside
You only know what you're told
Like a statue on a shelf
Boxed, wrapped, and sold

Nobody knows the feelings I hide
You only see a character I portray
Like a bird in a cage
I let my freedom go astray

Nobody knows what I had to give up
You only see the glory
Like taking a walk down a city street
Someone always hounding you for a story

Nobody knows how lonely it is
You only know what you read
Like being afraid to say I love you
Trying to distinguish it from greed

Nobody knows how hard I'm working
You only hear how much I'm making
Trying to be remembered for my songs
Not ripped jeans and my body shaking

Nobody knows what the future holds
You only hope for the best
Like ending all hunger
And putting all wars to rest

Joanne M. Yobak
Myrtle Beach, SC

From Hell to Heaven

I died and went to Hell last night
I cried *No!* at the dark sight
    At dawn's first sunbeam
    I awoke from dream
    And eyed our Savior Christ, the Light!

Ollie V. Zoller
Amarillo, TX

I was born February 16, 1931, between Reydon and Cheyenne, OK. My daddy Andrew Freeny Saunders was a Church of Christ preacher. My mama Cora Florence was homebound with four boys and six girls. I graduated from Pryor High School. Also I received a diploma from Long Ridge Writers Group. On June 2, 1952, I married William Eugene Zoller, World War II and Korean Conflict veteran. We were blessed with one boy, three girls, and two grandsons. Bill died July 3, 1989, from a self-inflicted 410 hunting rifle bullet through his hurting heart. Feeling blue, July 3, 2016, I wrote "From Hell to Heaven."

Jenny Dear

My love is on the shore,
  but something called me to the sea.
And as I write this epic, Jenny dear,
  I'll think of that last kiss
  you gave me.
I never felt a sting,
  for any who loved me;
  I've never looked back to see
  if anyone watched me leave.
But I felt amiss, and I looked back to see,
  as I left you, Jenny dear, Jenny dear!
  I always stopped the sun from risin'
  and pondered how it could have been different.
Now the waters are up to my chin,
  the regrets have begun, the sharks nibble at my feet —
  I take the liberty and libation
  from those sweet lips of yours, Jenny dear.
I know I'm sinning, if I spend an eternity
  in remembering that last kiss you gave me,
  Oh Jenny, Jenny dear!
  But before I go under,
  just one more kiss, for Johnny,
  Jenny dear!

Lonnie Bailey
Pineville, WV

Soul Builders, Soul Savers

Closing the last leaf of a treasured book, which gave
cause to raise my soul to universal heights, to open
every portal of my being to joy, hope, and pure
wonderment. That which leaves my breast filled with
awe... I am revived for having consumed it.
Rich with nutrients that feed my inner being, with
groans of ecstasy...

Unlike the cardboard garbage of cheap words filled
with phony explicatives that only give view to the
failed parentage of a hopeless being.

Thanks be to God for the soul builders. Inspired poets
and authors who create a masterpiece with their
knowledge, courage and gifted arrangement of words,
which give meaning to life, even among the very worst
egregious circumstances... to the very heights of
eternal felicity.

Abandoning any use of filth filled words, that are
slimy barnacles, which hold hostage the spirit and
suffocates it.

While these be few, those who can illuminate the great
horrors of life, while giving flight to our empyrean
dreams with the stroke of their pen, leaving us in tact.
Hail to the soul savers.

Marsha A. Perkins
Cedar City, UT

Autumn

A delightful season autumn can be,
From declining heat, sets you free.
Between summer and wintertime,
Celebrate autumn's bounty while prime.

A period of maturity for squash great,
Pumpkins and apple dishes to fill your plate.
Asters, goldenrod, ragweeds and mums
Bloom as the woodcutter's chainsaw hums.

Time to paint, caulk and proceed to repair,
Getting ready for winter's cold crisp air.
Goblins, ghosts and costumes so hairy,
Spooky sounds that to children are scary.

Great migrations are taking their place,
Seek warmer apparel, as air chills the face.
Locust and squirrels give us some clues,
While gorgeous leaves appear in all hues.

Football games, hot dogs and marching bands
Send signals of autumn across the lands.
Pathways covered with windswept leaves,
Reminders of autumn's beauty nature weaves.

Patricia A. Amburgey
Wichita, KS

As Far as I Could Tell, Life Was Good

As far as I could tell, life was good
Things were in place as they should
Went for my mammogram today
Things happened in the usual way
Two days later I got a call on my cell
My life had just gone to hell
The next thing I knew they did a sonogram
And before I knew it, a biopsy exam
I never understood, *Your life flashes before you*
But it does, in real time, too
The doctor scheduled a lumpectomy for 10
I couldn't wait for it to be over by then
The more you worry the worse it gets
Not only for you, the whole family frets
I woke up in recovery feeling for my breast
It was there, that feeling was the best
The doctor arrived with a smile on her face
"Your all clear," she said, I felt I was back in the human race
We'll know for sure in a week's time
I felt like my life was back to rhyme
The waiting was the hardest thing
You put your life on hold waiting for the phone to ring
The doctor said, "You are now cancer free"
To my surprise I screamed, "Yippee"
I didn't need chemo or radiation
My world is now in celebration

Dianne J. Hauser
Cincinnati, OH

Season of the Poll-parrots

Something's not good in the nation-hood
In the balance of the lesser evil, two must compete
The ballot is the poll-parrot's sought-after food

Perpetual squawking and image preening, quotas to meet
Mounds of green feed, all to buy ambition and power
In the balance of the lesser evil, two must compete

Soon the mud flies spreading the lies to grow and flower
The glowing eye spreads the poison far and wide
Mounds of green feed, all to buy ambition and power

Truth and logic quickly drown in the rising tide
In the sheeple herd silent despair, no one cares
The glowing eye spreads the poison far and wide

The green masters chortle in their private lairs
The balance quickly tips as the season finds its end
In the sheeple herd silent despair, no one cares

Finally a poll-parrot is chosen as the one to send
The balance quickly tips as the season finds its end
Something's not good in the nation-hood
The ballot is the poll-parrot's sought-after food

David R. Huff
Auburndale, FL

The poem is written in the terzanell form. Note the interlocking lines and rhymes. I have written and published two poetry books; the terzanell is the prevalent form used. Terzanell poems are ideal for story telling. This form of poetry is suited for experienced writers who wish a long poem.

Eyes

Eyes, are they really truth glares?
Or have they learned to lie at every turn?
The mirror can get blurry at times.
So many can fool you from time to time.
It makes you feel humiliated when you seek what you find.
The eyes to the soul have fooled many people today.
So the old saying should be changed.
Everything is upside down.
Flip the switch so you can find the mirror is really inside.
Don't trust your feelings anymore because you can be tricked
   and burned.
So the truth about eyes can confuse you now.
In fact they can make you feel like a clown.
The circus of life is not always a ride.
Some times it's a terrible ride.
Other times the wild mouse is a lot more fun.
The twist and turns are more sharply jerking you up and down.
Don't trust the roller coaster ride.
Being upside down is worse than the slide.
Hit a few balls, catch a few high flies, jump to the beat of a
   different drummer.
You'll find you'll have a much better summer.
Going backwards is not the answer.
To advance forward you have to learn to dance.
Ducking can be a safe answer too.
Find the real you!

Eleanor Pearl Atzert
West Palm Beach, FL

A Soldier's Letter

As the wars still rage on in this world,
I walk through the smoke and fire trying my best to make sense
of it all.
Thoughts of you keep me fueled,
so that I can continue to keep marching on.
A vision of your eyes hovers before me,
encouraging me to focus on the right path.
I yearn to be within your loving arms,
and I hunger to have your lips press against mine.
Being apart from you tortures my heart,
but the pain gives me the strength to fight on,
until the day comes where we will be united again.
I love you with all my heart and soul, and there is no sunrise
nor sunset
that can be compared to your beauty.
The special memories that we have shared together keep me alive
and fill me full of the hope of coming back home again,
to create even more wonderful ones with you!
I long to hear your sensual voice, as it has always put my mind
to ease,
especially after a long hard day
I wish to be in your arms, dancing to our favorite song,
under a full moon and a starlit sky.
Until that day, my love, remember that I live for you
and that I always shall to the end of time!

With sincere love,
Your Soldier of Freedom

Richard Stecher
Quakertown, PA

About the Rain

Some say it's drab and ugly
when it falls down from the sky.
They say its dull and gray and
they wish that it were dry.
Most say it makes them sad,
some even say they cry.
I'm glad it's them — not I.

It sparkles as it gently falls,
glistening in the air,
and brightens up the atmosphere
for all of those who care.
It brings the flowers to life
and clears away the smog.
With sun it forms a rainbow
in a cloud of fog.

Let it rain!
Let it pour!

Sher Lyckman
Orange, CA

Many years ago, while sitting in a restaurant waiting for friends to meet up for an impromptu trip to Las Vegas, I watched as the rain was pouring down outside. I thought about how most people feel about rain and how differently my friend, Peggy Ann, and I feel about it. We just love the rain and relish in the good times we have spent inside watching and listening to the it. On restaurant napkins, I wrote this little ditty, "About the Rain." She took the napkins from me and returned the poem to me printed on fine paper and framed as a gift on my next birthday. I just reminisce about our times and memories of days spent long ago with Peggy, Monica, and Judy on a road trip in pouring-down rain.

Race Against Time

The Red the White and Blue
We are all the same it's true
Reverse the tide remember the cost
We are all the same it's true
Etched in stone we pay it forward
Together we set the future's tone
Hand in hand together we stand
We are all the same it's true
Back to back
I've got yours
And you've
Got mine!

Scott J. Anderson
Milford, CT

Added to this poem was a blue ribbon. This poem was written for all the police officers so they may know they are appreciated and thought of as a tremendous asset to all communities. Also, I would like to mention the book of poetry I wrote, When Words Collide, *and a teenage sci-fi,* Net Force Ten.

Cycle

The sun arose with blinding light upon the sleepy earth
Its warmth of love caressed the hills and flushed the summer birth
It lured the seedlings from their bed in spiraling ascent,
To taste the kisses of the sun radiantly content.

All around the creatures rose and frolicked in their play
Flowers dressed in pretty clothes to join the blessed day;
Sun and Earth entwined their hands as lovers often do.
All creation craned their necks to see the scenic view.

But as the heat of summer passed, fond hopes began to fade.
The sun released the grip of love and left the earth in shade;
To camouflage her saddened face she donned a vivid robe.
Bright reds and yellows everywhere covered her abode.

The golden leaves left their perch and fluttered to the ground,
Her nakedness for all to view, a squalid little mound;
And so it was that love had lived and left the earth again.
As she slept 'neath winter white; she dreamed of what had been.

Wayne Firestone
Dubuque, IA

America

Upraised with infinity an outworking of blessing is at work
The cloud of silence is marching forward to eternal peace
As blue, red, and white simultaneously cross the sea
Leaving behind sunflowers and dreams in the effect
As water wears away stones nonetheless, history goes
Succeeding in the spiritual battlefield
Of hidden things unknown to the heart
Moving the decisive blow of victory
With a small sling and mighty faith
To save the one being held at the door post of the human mind
Where things kept fixed on time and location
Stripped away from the hexagonal prism the rays of his memory
Infinite silence clustered in the thoughts of the world
Oh, magnitude of gain knowable to infinity
Why did you forget to move endlessly?
Serenity of being given to creation a helping hand
Descending slowly, giving, transforming above and below
A synaptic pruning new life of grace as the seasons of the earth
Soaring high on wings of eagles I will make America great again
You have heard these things, look at them all
I will display my splendor with vigilance and justice
Descending to proclaim that which is true and eternal
Certainly I will melt away before the sunflower field
But I am still there carved toward greatness
To gladden the heart and brighten the soul of blue, red, and white
God bless America above the average on Earth.

Geoconda T. Berman
Aptos, CA

Aunt's Day

A day well spent with someone special
A day filled with fun
A day filled with joy
A day filled with peace
A day filled with love
A day filled moments of happiness
A day filled like a pot of gold, at the end of a rainbow!
Aunts are special people
An aunt is making special moments with someone dear to your
heart
Happy Aunt's Day!

Debra L. Bender
Medford, WI

Autumn Days

As my hair turns into autumn grays,
I'm grateful for all my summer days.
Now I am older, but I still celebrate what
it means to be alive.
And my youthful innocence I did
survive.
Now I have made it into these older days.
Now I bask in the halls of wisdom's ways.

Derek Walsh
Millis, MA

The Day We Married

The day we married the world
was moist with soft rain.
It began as soon as we said *I do*.
It was always so much, so
very much to me, to be married
and also to him.
And in looking back, although I
am without him now, I find
so much in my heart to feel,
that to God I bow, and remember
my vow, and how we kept
it to the end. From the
beginning on the day we married
he was always my dearest friend.
He will be with me in spirit until my very end.
It is as it was in my heart,
on our day, a feeling that
has never gone away. A feeling
of belonging to someone, and in quite a deep way,
that, although I am alone, I
carry that feeling still today.
And I pray this feeling
will stay and never pass away.

Heather Hardy
State College, PA

My Answer to Gossipers

What do I do?
You really want to know?
I dehydrate water
And ship to where the supply is low
They just add water and watch it flow
What do I do?
You really want to know?
I'm the star of silent radio
What do I do?
You really want to know?
I march in a parade while playing a piano
If my answers are quite bewildering
Actually I park cars atop the Empire State Building
The moral of this poem?
It goes to show
You won't know more than you need to know

Marvin D. Goldfarb
Sunnyside, NY

Mama Ramone

Carefully and exuberantly passing away
Under her soiled bed sheets
As she violently grasps the embedded threads
That embroider her shadowy, withered figure

Barbarically clenching her yellowed front teeth
As the agonizing promise of infinite death
Slumbers soundly and comfortably
Upon her deaf sense

Continuously evading the boisterous winds
Of a silent, molten graveyard
That cordially rumbles beneath her body
Giddily and vehemently awaiting the final words of her sentence

Shivering with wicked delusions
And obnoxiously flinching at the scratching iron
She lightly crossed paths with her vast memories
Of a life before no more
One of which did not include
The sad and broken tone
Of little, old Mama Ramone

Aaron Jacob Ozee
Addison, IL

Aaron Ozee is a best-selling American poet and the author of nine nationally recognized collections of poetry, including best-selling work Ironic Perfection: Poetic Works of Aaron Ozee. *Aaron has been featured in many prominent magazines and by countless leading news sources for his success in the publishing industry. In 2015, Aaron claimed a total of six world records for achievements as an author and entrepreneur with titles including his most important record, "Most Books Published by a Teenager." Aaron continues to push onward in his career and hopes that one day this world, as we know it to be, sees the beauty in his work the same way he does.*

Flowers

What would the world be without flowers?
Blooms of color more than a rainbow can show
And blossoms that promise a fruit to grow
The eyes behold & enjoy the beauty of them all
Some blooms are picked and used for medicine
Birds and bees feed on the blooms' nectar
Bees pollinate the blossoms for fruit to develop
Petals are pressed from the most fragrant blooms
To make precious cologne and exotic perfumes
Some plants bloom; we call them weeds
Often pulled before they go into seeds
We watch for a little rosebud to unfold
Oh yes, what would we do without flowers in the world?

Wie weare die Welt ohne Blumen im Garten?
Mit Farben mehr als wir vom Regenbogen erwarten
Blueten die uns Frucht gewarehren
Man schaut und beglueckt sich an dem Schoenen
Manche Blueten gepflueckt zu medizinischen Gebrauch
Voegel und Blenen naehren am Blueten Nektar Schmauss
Die Bienen polinieren die Blueten fuer Fruechte zu gedeien
Gepresste Bluetenblaetter fuer Cologne und Parfuemerien
Einige Pflanzen bluehen, als Unkraut bekannt
Und bevor sie zur Saat kommen, von der Erde gerammt
Wir schauen wie ein kleiner Rosenkopf zur Bluete kommt
O ja, was wuerden wir tun ohne die vielen Blumen in der Welt?

Margarete Lisa Flatebo
Ophir, OR

My father Max Dietrich was an artist with paints, words, and music. I am happy to have inherited some of his talents.

Purlieu

A large canvass on the coffee table
unframed, the work not mine
but helps to keep the heat away
in the seasonal humid summertime

Merely glancing as I am passing
antique auto stuck in snow
which covered almost everything
including fond memories of long ago

K27 now long retired
my mount now balking at the downhill ride
unanticipating the upward mountain
nor schuss Arapahoe Basin's slip slide and glide

As I roll my eyes slowly upward
to complete my run returning back
I glance at the iced, cold painting
purposeful pendulum to now meet its slack

Marilyn Winter
Toms River, NJ

Fireflies

They float dreamily through the summer night,
Across a soft, sky-lit sunset of red,
And their backs glow with a green-colored light.

A fire in the woods is burning so bright;
Now that the true heat of the day has fled,
They float dreamily through the summer night.

From the trees in the forest they take flight,
Moving towards the shore of the lake instead,
And their backs glow with a green-colored light.

Flying further now — intrigued by the sight
Of the cabin where their travels have led —
They float dreamily through the summer night.

A bright full moon gently bathes them in white,
As they fly past a window by the bed,
And their backs glow with a green-colored light.

They circle through the air as we sleep tight,
Now dreaming of the cooler days ahead.
They float dreamily through the summer night,
And their backs glow with a green-colored light.

Thomas Koron
Grand Rapids, MI

I was born in Grand Rapids, MI, on May 19, 1977. I have attended Northview High School, Grand Rapids Community College, Aquinas College, and Western Michigan University. I have always had a strong passion for poetry. I believe that poetry is more than just simply words written or printed on a page. It is an actual living, breathing entity that has the ability to change our lives. It is capable of painting a vivid portrait of any subject, emotion, or moment in time. These are the elements of poetry that make it truly immortal.

Four Ways to Look

If you are struggling with a problem
Look up to find your way
God is always in the picture
Just remind yourself to pray!

If you are faced with fear and wonder
Look back to see the past
God has always been there for you
And His blessings come on so fast!

If you are overwhelmed with sadness
Look forward and think of the good
God will teach you what you need to learn
By doing what you know you should!

Opportunities come from problems
Look within to draw on your faith
You will gain a new perspective
Using your faith to keep you safe!

Elva Dunham
Lodi, OH

I was inspired to write this poem on the day before a family member died while under hospice care. Our daughter and granddaughter are both hospice registered nurses who care for the very sick with love and compassion. It takes a very special individual to devote their nursing skills to this type of work. I admire their dedication, which is a special gift from God. I wrote this poem in their honor.

My Butterflies

Fly my sweet butterflies, fly high.
Please don't let your dreams pass you by.
Be the very best you can in every single way.
Let the sun dance upon your sweet little face
And the honeysuckles be the best you ever did taste.
Run through the fields without a care in the world.
You are my chocolate, all I want is much more.
Let all your dreams take you away from here.
I've always told you, you deserve the very best, my dears!
Learn to love every single chance you can get.
Don't go through this life with nothing but regrets.
Laugh as much as you can at all the little things.
Maybe one day you'll understand what it truly means.
I want the very best for all of you.
Because no one loves you as much as I do.

Jessica Lynn Knight
Clinton, SC

Untitled

She hates the rocks that cover the wall.
She cannot see their beauty.
She's missed the pattern that's
pressed into the stone.
Each is unique. Each is its own.
The artist that built the spectacular wall
matched each with such perfection.
It takes an artist's eye
to make the right selection.

Sometimes I close my eyes
and think of my dear mother.
Her loving, gentle voice I hear
is sweet and like no other.
Many years have passed away.
Today I have turned 90,
but in my head, mind, and soul,
a child I'll be and not turn old—
because of the love that was shown to me,
a wonderful, sweet memory.

Carol Geddes-Lynnet
La Mesa, CA

In Memory of John S. and John T.

Recently I received a telephone call
About the death of my brother, John.
It was difficult for me to hear,
About a relative I had and loved for so long.
We grew up in a small Iowa town,
And the other John did, too.
He became my husband for 42 years;
Both are now in Heaven.
I remain happy, but also blue.
Some days I want to phone them and talk
Or go on a long eventful walk.
I know they have a heavenly, Christian life,
Without pain or any strife.
That doesn't mean my memories of them
Leave complete belief that everything is fine,
But life with our Christ Jesus should bring a joyful time!

Nan Tebrinke
Carmel, IA

Life Is a Challenge

What is life all about?
We all know life is a challenge
As we can see.
We all have problems;
Some are small problems,
And we can handle them.
Others are big problems,
And they are to figure out,
What will I do?
I need my friend, or someone
I can talk to, to help me out.

What a bright tomorrow it will be.
I will never forget my friend,
It all worked out the way I wanted it to.
I am a different person as you can see.
It put a smile on my face.
Life is worth living.
I know that my problems will be solved,
And I feel great because of that.

Loretta Aul
Belle Vernon, PA

Humanities

I found out that my sanity is wrapped with ease,

Knowing that God has written my history.

As I live to learn that my love for
music defines my philosophy,

Being reborn, collectively being Mastered
as I embrace my story,

It is now that I understand with
pride and dignity,

The Lord had mercy with kindness and
blessed us with his generosity.

In consideration, always be grateful to
goodness and kindness,

Just because only here you'll find this,
Humanities!

Tunder Davis
Jonestown, MS

The Terminator

Be aware of your surroundings.
Listen carefully to promised words.
A plan was set from the beginning of time
To destroy us all; martial law is set to go.

Think it strange how he has no emotion.
He knows our country will fall.
He has planned to take us all down.
Key cells of the enemy are waiting;
They are listening for his command.

Cry out to your creator.
Sound the alarm for all to draw near.
Jesus our promised Redeemer
Has won the battle for all.
Lift up your hands and rejoice.
Your redemption is drawing nigh!

Sally B. Ray
Palestine, TX

Creek Bed

I walk a long-distance smile
beneath dream-draped trees
and raft another slow mile
after wind-tamed waters beam back at me.

Sunbathed blue eyes petal-close
cooling down to the smooth rock-gliding flow
of leaf-drummed life, quivering sound
and insight rivering 'round

like this clay-bellied creek, light in tow
slightly shivering as it comes and goes.
I think I may have traced here —
worry-free and currently clear —

a place to lift a dead spirit or one dying
to rest and peace like headstone sleep or simply flying,
spurring a recording mind to pause and play where
a heart is always home and burns to stay there.

Ray Wolbert
Elyria, OH

Who Jesus Is

Jesus is the Savior of the world.
He is Christ the Anointed
He is Lord to govern.
He is the Leader to guide
And Captain to conquer.
Jesus is all right.

He is the beginning and the end.
He is the first and last.
He is right now and He's after a while.
He's History;
He is the present and the future.
He's yesterday, today, and tomorrow.

He is the shortest distance
Between two points.
He is the decimal point
Between time and eternity.
He's louder than the sounds
And swifter than speed.
He's older than age — better than good;
He's all universal.

Fred Cato Jr.
Casa Grande, AZ

Three-Fold Cord

It was just yesterday
That I held you in my arms
Looking innocent and fragile,
Elated to hear your first cry.

Man invented the pacifier
And it happened to be close by,
Then I noticed why you were crying;
All I could say was my, my, my.

Learning from our early struggles
Teaching us to have a strong mind,
Adapting to life's challenges
We can sing sweet by and by.

The Lord has been our shepherd
As He has been throughout the years.
Through cloudy days and stormy nights
He faithfully wipes our tears.

Leaping faith is like a bungee jump,
Except the trust is in the Lord.
My Son, please hear my plea:
All the Trinity to be
Your three-fold cord.

Jose Hernandez
Donna, TX

Raising a family without the Lord's help is super tough. It seems that the more we try to raise our children in the Lord's way, the more they drift apart. Our prayer is that before it is too late, all children seek the Lord's face.

He Left Me Still His Wife

This year's been very hard for me
I lost the love of my life,
But God took him up in Heaven
And he left me still his wife.

I finally know what love is
My heart is telling me,
Throughout my life I loved one man,
If you know me you can see.

We spent so many years together
With children, pets and things.
It's very hard to express the loss
And what sadness it brings.

We did most things together;
It's very hard to believe.
And I never thought at any time
That one of us would leave.

I tell this story once again
So I may finally heal
And let my memories fill me up
So happiness is what I'll feel.

MaryLou Lehrke Arnold
San Diego, CA

This poem was written in remembrance of my husband of fifty-seven years. I have nothing but good memories of our years together. We have five children, twelve grandchildren, and soon-to-be-eight great-grandchildren. I am very lucky to have such wonderful memories. I've been very blessed even though my heart is breaking. I love having this opportunity to express my feelings and go forward. Thank you, Eber & Wein!

Untitled

Love comes not from within the mind,
But from within the heart.
For it is there that is stored the pain
And torment of reality.
For love without pain
Is like a rose without sunshine.

It just doesn't exist.

Stephen David Hart
Ojai, CA

Be What You Want to Be, but Be Yourself

Be careful, but strong.
Be smart, but courageous.
Be able, but intelligent.
Be kind, but sweet.
Be trustworthy, but wise.
Be lucky, but cool and smart.
Be mindful, but thinking ahead.
Be remarkable, but brilliant.
Be righteous, but spiritful.
Be what God would have you to be, but very thankful.
Be all you can be, but be yourself.

Darlene Brown
Chesapeake, VA

Steffi

Seldom does he, does anyone, have the chance
to move through their closing days in such lively, bright
company, to dance
in step to music that only a lifetime of dark and light
could compose,
one shorn of lullabies to be sure, no hymns either
to offer thanksgiving or praise
in her early days,
only the daily, tuneless beat of survival
mixed now, in the last decade,
with high-stepping, inspiring stuff, a revival
that puts her past on its heels
and lets her toes tap themselves
to a new, love-driven place.
Her life has become an art,
a miracle in the making as his dear friend
and teammate,
taking on the old to create the new,
reflects her honors degree in life's school
of dance,
mastering and teaching those moves
that set us free,
swirling, whirling, to be sure,
but in the center's eye that perfect peace,
her fire and grace lead us to.

Robert Skeele
Laconner, WA

The Evil of Man

I am the displeasure of man,
bringing forth harm and misfortune.
I am the disobedient child,
craving his mother's attention.
Danger and lies guide my unlawful actions,
as I spread hate and sickness across the world.
I am death and destruction.
I am misery and pain.
I am all things bad yet disguised in so much beauty:
Lust, gluttony, greed, sloth, wrath, envy and pride.
I am the evil of man.

Samantha Price
Ellington, MO

Getaway Day

My son and I have lived in this house many years
But it is, or so appears
We speak in different tongue
I speak *Mom* and he speaks *Son*
Somehow or other we figure it all out
And find out what each other is about
When the outside world starts closing in he'll say
Let's make this a "getaway" day
So we go to shop and dine
Then we understand each other fine

Elizabeth Thompson
Blandburg, PA

Mother's Day Split in Two

Mother's Day was our day split in two,
with half for me and half for you.
First as a mom then as a daughter,
bringing a yellow rose in a vase of salt water.

Now celebrating Mother's Day
isn't the same since you went away.
Our day we no longer split in two,
with half for me and half for you.

I still get my half, this is true;
gone is the half just for you.
No yellow rose in a vase of salt water,
since you've gone I'm no longer a daughter.

The day God took you far, far away,
forever changed my Mother's Day.
Mother's Day, our day, split in two
with half for me and half for you.

Now it's just my day with a little laughter
and a day with a few tears after.
Mother's Day is a day I split in two,
with half for me and half for you.

Debra DeVeney
Ione, CA

Ye Old Recliner

Bought when new
For dear old Dad in his 80s.
My how time flew…
Dad was supposed to sit, watch TV
Even growth of daisies.

Great-grandsons love to sit in it.
They press lever to move it forward,
Back and up and down.
Grandpa began to stay in his hospital
Bed and watched birds in the feeder.
He wasn't worried about the electric meter.

We share a bowl of peanuts
And one-half peeled apple for a treat.
He sleeps four-hour naps,
Then does nebulizing treatments — machine
Prepared by family members.

He enjoys TV game shows and in the
Evening laughs at reruns of *Everybody Loves Raymond*.
Grandpa likes his back scratched,
Left, right, up, down.

Old friends and family visitors come
As I sit in his recliner chair.

Bonnie Neuman
Evart, MI

*Father's Day, June 15, 2014, I became a widow. My husband was eighty-three,
and we cared for him at home for four years. This poem was written in his memory.*

At the Speed of Mind

Ideas fly like musical notes played.
Amazing plans form as bricks are laid.
Building a network, he shares his gift.
Children absorb them. Their lives soon shift.

He can't control it. Goodness always a goal.
With the young and the old, he fills their soul.
Their music begins flowing as characters grow.
Positive, power vibrations! Movements never slow.

Sweeping up children with musical brooms,
He nurtures and guides them as through life he zooms.
And when the dusty melodies finally do settle,
He has made them better with drums and metal.

Composing a life symphony, no score is too much.
Enhancing the worlds of all he can touch.
Schemes and dreams continually spin and unwind.
And so goes this man..traveling at the speed of mind.

Tina Stoneking-Trujillo
Taos, NM

Music teacher, Mr. Eric Reed Stoneking, inspired this poem as he keeps music alive in schools and with our seniors. His programs have reached hundreds of children each year. The teacher-inspired non-profit hornsinhand.org keeps repairing and purchasing instruments for those who might miss experiencing a lifelong gift of music. His adult and senior bands support this non-profit (a win on many levels). Mr. Stoneking's enthusiasm captivates and inspires music appreciation at a time when we cannot afford to lose it. Like poets, we cannot have too many musicians.

By Their Works Shall Ye Know Them

Blood-drenched sand yields no crops
Knows no race or nationality
Slaughtered children stare wide eyed into Heaven
Mothers, daughters savaged
Their temples violated, mutilated with warrior atrocities
Who sow them with seeds death will not sprout
Love crucified by hate
Forgiveness and mercy brought to its knees
Crying out to a merciful God before a God without mercy
A God who delights in the destruction of all man has built
Even to the temple of the soul
In whose kingdom will the bullets rest?
In whose kingdom will the executioner stand?
Upon what principle will butchered innocence and genocide
    be raised?
Between the bullets and the bombs rains the blood
Bodies and bones crushed into the dust from whence they came
Into what was once Eden
While beneath the sun's eye, demons of darkness
Drink their fill, dance their murders
Defiant to the end
The storm is coming just for them
God will not be defamed! God alone creates
Demons only desecrate
By their works shall ye know them

Paula Compo-Pratt
Westville, NJ

Close to Him

We wander away doing our own thing;
We willfully walk the wrong paths in life.
We make mistakes, errors in judgment;
Fall short of God's will.
Sin.
Good news!
God is the God of second chances.
When we play the Prodigal Child
Amidst all of life's turmoil
God calls to us.
Along life's pathways
God lovingly looks for us.
His goal is to find us,
Bring us home,
Willingly take us back.
God is our Heavenly Father.
So, let us stand still;
Pause quietly;
Hear His sweet, soft voice!
God's desire is for us to be close to Him.
He wants to share His love with us.
After all, He is the God of second chances.
Let us be close to Him!

Bill M. Watt
Fayetteville, NC

I wrote this to celebrate the occasion of my sister Cheryl Rae (Watt) McGraw's eternal birthday on July 3, 2016, when she committed her life to Christ Jesus in Chickasha, OK. She was saved for eternity with our heavenly Father! Knowing that Satan will work hard to dissuade her from her decision to become a Christian, I wrote this poem as an encouragement to and for her as well as everyone who wants to follow Jesus as their Lord and Savior.

The River of Time

There is a river of time
When thoughts stream back across the years
Along the banks of the river of life.

Guiding out boat together as one,
Journeying through the shallows and rapids and still waters,
We kept our boat afloat.

What we have seen!
What we endured!
The good times we've had together!

And now we sit by the bank of the river of life,
With fire aglow, closer to our destination,
With memories of the past.

Ready for the final run
In the river of life (what fun!)
Yes! You and I, a team of one.

And we know, love and care (despite the jolts)
Have kept our boat afloat;
We journey together,
We journey together as one.

Kenneth Swan
Marion, IN

Wartime Heros

The parades and flag waving, stuff like that to see
means nothing at all, nothing at all to me.
It's the soldiers and sailors who performed in strife, by gee!
Paying their ultimate price; that and that alone won the victory!

Men who fought and died in zero weather and colder
Those men, their valor, their heroism… none have been bolder!
Men whose war-torn bodies lie in Washington, DC, Tomb of the
    unknown Soldier
Their bravery, their bloodshed causes me to weep and moan
Their sacrifice, bravery, valor I applaud, and that alone!

Also their buddies who came home with limbs blown off—
We owe them so much, lying in VA hospitals, bodies in pain.
These overwhelming thoughts cause me to wonder about the gain
Only these young men knew; to me war seems so insane!

Maybe we should cut the nonsense of Fourth of July and
    November 11th parades.
Instead, invest those gas dollars to VA hospitals for soldiers' aide.
Let's support our suffering heros who lie in beds of pain.
Let's support them over and over again from any of our
    wealthy gain.

Anna Schuler
Broken Bow, NE

I am a retired nurse. I have been a substitute Sunday school teacher. I was born in Rock County, NE. I worked in a law office after high school graduation. I am the mother of three, grandmother of four, and great-grandmother of six.

National Parks in Western United States

It is love of our national parks that I want to convey
For these national parks have a lot to show and say
Glacier National Park has lots of glaciers and trails
Yellowstone has wildlife, geysers, sites, and waterfalls
Zion has picturesque vistas and deep canyons
Bryce National Park has hoodoos and colorful sands
Rocky Mountain has mountains and elk that roam
Even out of the park into the town we call home
Utah has Moab, Capital Reef and Cedar Breaks to see
South Dakota has Mt. Rushmore to remind you and me
Of the great fathers of this great land
And also has a monument for Custer's Last Stand
The Grand Tetons stand tall and regal
Grand Canyon has all colors and is home of the eagle
In Washington, there stand the Cascades
Down further, there is the beautiful Yosemite
And who can forget the beautiful park and Sequoia tree
There are other national parks I've yet to explore
But I have found peace and beauty in all these parks
Serenity in all of them and more

Beverly D. Harris
Sun City, AZ

Land

It's strange how one piece of land
calls out to you and you know you're home.
You never like to venture too far from it or
stay gone too long.
It's actually just a piece of dirt like
all other land.
It's like when you're gone until you
get back, you really can't breathe well
until you're home again and your land you see,
It makes me wonder, do I own the land or
does the land own me?

Bonnie Watson Jolly
Cedartown, GA

Memory Files

When all the trees wear October dress
And winter still is sleeping,
My dreams of summer go to rest
And memories start creeping
Of springtime flowers and summer's glow,
Of warmth of sun and showers.
I while away my autumn days and bask in golden hours.
When winter comes, I'm all prepared,
I've stored my memories well,
And I can pull them out of files
When winter blues impel.

Cora Irene Crews
Bloomington, IL

Reaching Out

Oh, Lord! What has happened to our nation?
Have we forgotten our relation?
Have we forgotten some of the important things?
Oh what our prayers can bring.

May we not forget who is on the throne.
That truly means we are never alone.
We need to pray you have Your way
To carry us through to another day.

Thank You for being there
So we may Your love share.
Open our hearts
That it may be a brand new start.

Darlene S. Gonser
Kendalville, IN

My Daughter

I loved her so,
But God our Father
Said she must go
To live with Him
In Heaven above
Where there she's safe
And surrounded with love
Thy will be done
We always pray
And yet we hope
For one more day
To spend our time
With those we love
Who's now an angel
Looking down from above
And I'll always love her
From far away
And hope to join her
This I pray.

Della Jean Shipley
Hoxie, KS

Friends I've Made Along the Way

As we live our lives from day to day
We meet many people along the way.
Some only for brief moments — maybe standing in line
Or others whose lives and ours entwine.
They've given smiles and hugs as they've passed my way
That have sometimes lifted or carried me along life's way.
Their cheery words and comfort I find
Have stayed securely in my heart and in my mind.
They share my laughter and my tears
And shall remain priceless throughout the years.
They give of their wisdom as well as their time —
And someday to others may I give some of mine.
And I wish to others all these gestures to share —
For these are qualities of friends who truly do care.
For ways they've touched my life and influenced the way
   I am today,
I am thankful for the friends I've made along the way.

Dianne Foushee
Sanford, NC

I am so blessed with friends — wonderful, close, hold-your-hand, listen-to-you, cry-with-you kind of friends! Think about the people you've come to know. I just tried to put it into words. Circumstances in life make you come in contact with possible lifetime friends.

Bank Audit

'Twas the night before audit
and all through the house
all the creatures were stirring and even the mouse.
The stockings were hung by the chimney with care
in hopes that the auditors soon would be there.
The president was all nestled and snug in his chair
while visions of profits danced in the air.
Dot in her kerchief and I in my cap
had just settled down for a long winter's nap,
when out on the lawn there arose such a clatter
we sprang to our feet to see what was the matter.
Away to the window we flew like a flash
tore open the shutter and threw open the sash.
And what to our wondering eyes should appear
but all of the auditors carrying their gear:
scuba and tanks and golf clubs galore,
looking for papers they looked at before.
Finally they left at the close of the day
picking and choosing what they would say.
Exceptions, exceptions, they shouted with glee,
glad they were done and finally set free.
Up on the rooftop to the courses they flew.
Dash away, dash away, my auditing crew.
I heard them exclaim as they rode out of sight,
Merry Xmas to all and to all a good night.
2 tickets for Florida, I want the next flight!

Helen A. Pesamoska
Venice, FL

Child of God

The mirror reflects her dead-eyed stare,
cheap rouge on her lips, and cheap dyed hair.
She has one feeling left; that feeling is clear.
On the inside, she cried with dried-up tears.

She was a child captured outside her school.
They hooked her on drugs; they used every tool.
They turned her out young to the vile and the scum.
They threatened her family; she's too scared to run.

They took her security, innocence, too.
They beat her and starved her; her chances are few.
She's scorned on the street; people haven't a clue.
They might show some mercy, if only they knew.

Janet Sue Deckard
Texas City, TX

At One with the Scarecrow

When you walk by the scarecrow at the edge
Of the farm borders, way beyond the hedge,
Don't be shocked at how real he looks since it's me,
And this shouldn't be surprising for you to see.
After life tore me up, an outer shell of me
Was all that was left,
A ghoul without breath —
A hollow man, all my insides have been removed
(The heart and soul weren't warranty approved).
My face is burnt and black, my eyes stare with black holes.
My ears cannot hear the ringing when the bell tolls.
I never smile now; I never smiled much before.
I didn't expect much from life and got nothing more.
I am like a dead man — dead to life, dead to all.
All my hope and joy is gone, my aims are small.
I have nothing to live for,
And excuses for staying are poor.
I am alone; my comrades are filthy crows
Who hover about my rags when the wind blows.
My whole life has been a joke, a mockery
Of real life, and now I am numb and empty
Of any spark, standing far out
In my eternal night of doubt
With a blank-face expression that doesn't care
And a thousand-mile-long stare
That peers afar off into despair.

Leo Weber
Livonia, MI

How Hot Is Hot?

It's so hot you actually can fry supper on
your car—although it should not be done.
   It is so hot, no matter how much liquid is
consumed, it is just not enough.
   It is so hot an ice cold glass of milk will
be sour if left out for five minutes.
   It is so hot, and this is the truth, it feels
as if my fingernails are melting.
   It is so hot the air shimmers and the
sidewalks glimmer.
   You know it's hot when air moved by fans
does nothing to cool sun-heated skin.
   It is so hot ice cubes disappear in a glass
almost before your drink is gone.
   It's so sunny hot, definitely it is not a
good idea to mow the lawn.
   It is so hot, by the time your last flower
bed is watered, the first bed is looking parched.
   It's so hot when hanging out clothes,
the first item is dry by the time
the last one is pinned on the line.
   It's so hot the worm on a fisherman's
hook wants to go for a swim!
   Hot, hot is when an ice cream cone is divine
even when it is dripping faster than it can be licked.
   You know it is hot when at 5:00 AM you are
already sweating up a storm.
   It is so hot, sticky skin and stringy hair are the norm.
   Cheer up, for in a few months, winter's chill will be here
to make us forget all about the heat of summer
and we will be shivering with frigid temps
to complain about!

Linda R. Dreyer
Cumberland, WI

Fluffy Clouds

Soft fluffy clouds float by,
On their way around the world,
Viewing the earth below,
As they tumble and swirl.

On their way around the world,
The wind plays with them,
As they tumble and swirl,
Those soft white pillows.

The wind plays with them,
As it blows in and through,
Those soft white pillows,
As they travel from our view.

As it blows in and through,
Soft fluffy clouds float by,
As they travel from my view,
This poem is through.

Linda Carmon
Cadillac, MI

Oriental Friend

If what we say is really true
that God keeps me but Buddha you,
Should we not then be worlds apart?
Yet I suspect we share one heart.

Do you not smell the rose as I
And watch the birds cross the sky?
Does music not delight your heart
And sorrow cause tears to start?

What mystic force beyond control
Made us to be kindred soul?

Lucy Clingan
Myersville, MD

For My Dad

A World War II veteran, so loyal and true,
He fought for his country, the Red, White, and Blue.
He did his best to be all he could be
As husband and daddy, brother and son —
As grandpa and uncle, caregiver for one.
But I'm not done, for you see
The list keeps going on and on.
A hard worker he was, and still to this day
He never gives up! It's just not his way!
With his wife by his side for 71-plus years,
They worked hard and played hard
To be all they could be.
His home is his castle (he never went too far away),
With lights that are dim
As he quietly sits and waits for the day
When, once again, he and his bride
Will sit side by side —
And watch the airplanes fly by!

Olivia Alban
Deer Park, WA

I grew up in Fresno, CA, with my older sister and my parents who worked hard all their lives. I lost my dad a little over a year ago. I know he is reunited with my mom and they are both still watching over me. I miss them both so much but know one day I will be reunited with them. Until that day comes, I will keep them busy!

Another Day

As dawn approaches turning darkness into light
the sun shines on the lake like diamonds
so clear and bright.

Another day of sunshine to
share with love and laughter,
another chance to make it right.

Will the sun shine brightly
in the sky or be hidden behind the clouds
leaving shadows to obscure the light?

Dusk comes quickly as the sun sets on the
horizon, turning daylight into darkness each night.
Waiting with anticipation, we marvel at the
sky softly glowing with shades of color
today, tomorrow, and forever, it feels so right.

Another moon is rising slowly.
Another dream is ours tonight.

Renette JoAn Colwell
Lake Almanor, CA

My Earthly Treasure

Eve
A woman whose grace
Whose tenderness
Whose beauty
Truly encompasses
Each component of a garden
The forget-me-nots
Carnations and roses
Sweet peas and lilies
Pansies and petunias
Daffodils and violets
Daisies and orchids
Tulips and sunflowers
All unique and lovely
In their own right
But not unique and lovely as Eve
Whose soul shines through her eyes

Robert I. Garcia
King City, CA

Come Sept 28th, I'll be eighty-five. Writing has become a good part of my life. This writing is the end. Eva is my book of poetry. She has now become my garden of rare flowers. I relate love and feelings for both the one I feel for and the flower I compare Eva with. Conclusion: I'm glad to be an American, happy to be an Indian poet.

Of Love Scorned

A love scorned is death un-adorned
In a forest left alone, beneath dead trees
Flowers to cushion my fall into my final sleep
Dressed to the hilt for my lover that killed
All the love within me; I am not pleased
For now I lie here, his love is my death
My soul is lost within this forest grave
Where no one can find me, except fallen tree debris
That has been shed over me for a decade you see
I have fallen upon a ground so hard
There is no way I can recover my heart
For it is lost forevermore to all who knew me
Before he brought me here to kill me
To be his own tragedy that he will have to carry
Beyond my open grave; beneath a deep blue sky
That will accept and love me, for me
Not what it wants me to see, and be

Ramona Quivonia Prak
El Cajon, CA

Life is so fragile and love is so delicate. We must learn to take others into our lives with care — never strangling the relationship to death before love can bloom, because once it is strangled and squashed to death, you may not recover the love once held by your spouse or lover.

What Does Help Mean?

It means not taking
control of someone's life,
body and soul.
  Giving them the word
when they need it,
  Giving of your time
if they need it,
  Giving them more than
a dime if they need it,
  Giving them help to
find shelter when they
need it,
  Giving yourself peace
of mind when you need it.

Lola Maire Boutte
Houston, TX

Today people say they want to help. They want to take over a person's life who just may need a little help or encouragement.

Nature Passing By

Beneath the feathers an eagle above
Soaring high into the sky
The powerful wind on which she climbed
Was nature passing by.

Upon the stripes, the zebra's fame
While grazing swatting flies
A sudden panic, then thundering hooves
Was nature passing by.

How thick, how beautiful the lion's mane
How courageous was his pride
And the weaker that he preyed upon
Was nature passing by.

But suddenly it ends!
There are no more zebra herds
Nor lion dens
No more eagles in our sky
We killed them without reason
As man passed nature by.

Suzanne A. Soucy
San Jose, CA

Autumn's Symphony: Andante Movement

Earth's concert hall quiets slowly—
 sounds are blended, rich colors abound—
 as the baton is lifted...

The *Violins*: ...rasping dried out stalks and leaves once green,
 stand sentinel, awaiting the noisy picker to rumble by,
 and pluck and snatch the dropped, turned wrong-side-to
 pockets richly crammed with golden coin.

The *Horns*: ...honking geese in flight formation,
 shattering the crisp blue sky
 in raucous wave, after wave, after wave.

The *Flutes* and *Reeds*: ...shrilling brazen maples
 shake their freshly frosted halos, their reddened carrot-tops,
 as brazen harridans scream, "Look at me! Look at me!"

The *Cellos* and the *Basses*: ...echo the land
 in groaning abundance, as garish pumpkins,
 and mufti-gourds resound their own
 ache and somber heralding,
 of each passing Indian summer day,
 of each rising harvest moon,
 of each rattling west wind's snare.

While the *Harp*: ...as newly raped fields,
 where soy's proliferance once flourished, now hushed,
 waits with grief's sweet relief and
 rests in poised adagio. Amen

Sister Mary K. Himens
Champaign, IL

As a professed religious woman, I have experienced a very rich and rewarding life of service—as a teacher, principal, parish worker, campus minister, and college professor. This listing does not include my many years as a psychotherapist in private practice. My poetry and other writings have been published in various journals, as well as my own volume of poetry. The poem above was inspired by my many trips along Illinois country roads in October and November.

Beautiful Butterflies

The beautiful colorful butterflies
Are every where
As they flutter their wings
And fly in the air

Some land on the beautiful
Red roses there
That were planted with love and care

The birds are singing and
Chirping away
They seem to be saying
What a beautiful day

Springtime is finally here
As the beautiful colorful butterflies
Flutter their wings and fly in
The air

Bobbi Jo Hager
Ozark, AL

Support Our Police

Our police are out there working
    protecting you and me
trying to keep our streets safer
    as everyone can see.
When they leave home each day
    their family is behind
just to serve and protect us
    their life is on the line.
Have you never stopped to think
    how this world will be
without them there to protect us
    from all of the misery?
There are people getting shot at
    every day of the week.
If we see something happening
    it is up to us to speak.
This can be our way of showing
    the police that we care
they are all out there working
    and can't be everywhere.
I lived in the Eighth District
    for almost thirty years.
When it comes to fighting crime
    they erased our fears.
Now when we're having trouble
    it's johnny on the spot
and take it from Cherokee Lee
    that really means a lot.

Cleatus Cherokee Lee Murdaugh
Chicago, IL

Spaceship of Zion

The spaceship of Zion is
heading to outer space
God knows we are coming
He prepared for us a place
Are you ready for that trip
beyond the sky?
Are you ready for the sweet
by and by?
We don't have to buy a ticket
Jesus paid the price
On the Cross of Calvary
He laid down his life
Are you ready for the journey
somewhere beyond the sky?
Our eternal home is waiting
in the sweet by and by
When He calls our number
we won't have time to wait
His loving arms wide open
at Heaven's gate
Are you ready for the journey
beyond the sky?
We will love forever
in the sweet by and by
God's celestial wonder and
eternal peace never cease

John Brannick
Colby, KS

Talking to God

I stayed awake all night and prayed
I knew that You were there
I didn't quite know what to say
Just knew that You would care
I feel like I'm broke in half
My heart is broken, too
Just don't have any answers
I still don't know what to do
Thought talking to You would help
You could really ease my pain
Maybe lighten my load a bit
So I don't feel like I'm all to blame
If You take time to listen
I'll give it one more try
I will fold my hands and pray
As I look up toward the sky
You may not have my answers
I'll guess only time will tell
At least I feel my load is lifted
By talking to You, it helps

Barbara Mader
Hoxie, KS

My family and I are going through a rough time right now. We have so many questions and so few answers. I've turned to God to help us; at least I feel better talking to Him.

Tom

Lord, I guess you needed him,
This very close friend of mine.
All of his friends and next of kin
Will miss Tom all the time.

He always worked so hard
Building homes for folks,
But also took the time
To enjoy a beer and tell some jokes!

All the good years that we shared
Working and raising a family,
He always showed he cared
And that was important you see.

When circumstances caused us to part,
I thought my world would shatter.
He always remained in my heart,
Keeping in touch was what really mattered!

Please ease all the aches and pain
For all of us left here,
Who will never be the same
With the loss of one so dear.

Daisyann B. Fredericks
Canajoharie, NY

Kindness Works

Many friends and neighbors I have known
Have now passed on.
I think of them from time to time
Though they are gone.
Now I don't know so many
And my circle's not so wide,
But my appreciation goes
To those who still abide.
Your goodness and your kindness
Is on what the world depends.
I'm blessed to know my neighbors
And my good, kind, loving friends.
Always in remembrance
I will hold the many perks
Of the kindness that was given,
And I tell you
Kindness works.

Carol Kaufman
Portland, OR

It's the Little Things I Miss

I miss your kiss and your touch
That I enjoyed so much
I miss your scent when I held you near
And whispered in your ear
I miss seeing you in your slumber cap
And you sitting on my lap
I miss seeing your face with a great big grin
When ordering any dessert you can imagine
I miss every little embrace
And the constant smile on your face
I miss all of these things it's true
But most of all, I just miss you

Chester Williams
Jewett City, CT

soulmate call

numbness of tipped fingers in this wild
where, how, when will a love, again as god's child?
a scream, shout out loud,
run through wind, the crisp of white whispers: now
a guess when ma hair's at large , when a touch the blue moon and a
dare to scratch birds fly south, trick ma being
a hear them chatting, very close to us seeing shit, that hurts but a
keep walking, keep wanting, keep demanding
freezing ma skin and blending ma sin is me:
hey? how u been and how much more
call ya now, can suffer no more a pretend a'm a human wore
haven't loved ya before,
but scream your name we're close and a am ready for your flesh,
fame and so much more feel me dripping and is fine
y'all keep writing, till ya find me and ya're mine rose quarts all
around ma neck,
a'm good to me even a sleep every other night in fish creek on the
deck were a'm god's special wreck
hungry for us, will feed each other from fruits and never let us pass
a draw frozen stars of happiness,
suddenly a'm happy
more then a ever thought , or anything a ever bought lips moist,
retracted to shelter
will report when called upon ya and ma own life director rip ma
flesh, snow will keep me safe
make love to me, no one will doubt this quest god's aware,
he'll send ya this christmas the only gift a've ever need: a confess

Nina Racila
Calgary, AB

In the Lagoon

That little boy
Standing by the lagoon
His shadow a tiny light
Cast across the water's edge

The silence of a gentle
Ripple, his innocence
A soft glow, he calmly
Saunters an inch too deep

A sudden wind, a slight
Ripple, the little boy
Shifts and in a misty
Moment fades into the marsh

So near the cries howl and rise
The shattered earth responds
How suddenly a little life
Has ebbed deep into the darkness
And now we only hear
The weeping of the moon

Corman Atkins
La Quinta, CA

Ol' Faithful

He was five minutes old when I saw him
standin' in a stall with his mama.
He was on his feet, his legs long and slim,
sprawled out and shakin' in every direction doing the mambo.

Mama was proud of her wonder of nature,
a perfect example of equine genealogy.
She'd do her best to raise, feed, and nurture.
Certainly he'd be in some cowboy's future.

He grew to be tall, sleek, and handsome,
for his cowboy he'd be quick, strong, and faithful.
He could sort, cut out, chase and then some.
He'd stare a big bull down and not be fearful.

We herded cows from Virginia Dale to Carter Lake,
checked yearlings all over two counties for gosh sake.
He would do what I needed in mud, rain, or shine.
For a job well done the pleasure was mine.

His registered name was Impressive and he sure was.
I just called him Ol' Faithful, you faithful pal of mine.

Rex A. Mannon
Loveland, CO

A Caregiver's Plight

Once bright, full of energy, loving life,
Now exists muddled in pain and strife,
With pills of a mysterious kind,
To numb the body and quiet the mind.
Small of stature, proportionate in size,
Pleasant countenance, questioning eyes,
Just a brief glimpse of the years gone by,
Only fleetingly, you can catch on the fly.
Empathy shown comes in moments rare,
As a harp's melody floating on air.
Tears you attempt to hide, so not to explain
The toll on your heart suffering ingrains.
Anger, frustration and feelings of despair,
Consume time and energy when you care.
Only faith in the one who answers prayer
Brings about welcome relief from the snare.

Joy Dockery Randall
Bryan, TX

I write this as a caregiver; writing about life experience has always been my therapy. I dedicate this with empathy for the caregivers of this world.

A Special Catch

One day as I was fishing, I looked up in a tree
To see a wise old owl staring down at me
"Hi There" he said, "Are you catching any fish?"
I looked up at him and replied, "No, but I wish"
Well, I'll help you, just give me some time
When I hoot, just pull in your line"
I waited and waited, then to my dismay
Came a very loud hoot, him saying, "There's one
coming your way"
I gave a big tug yelling, "He's on good and tight!"
He said, "It looks like you're in for a very good fight"
I pulled and reeled and got it to the bank
A nice-sized catfish, and looked up to thank
The wise old owl up in the tree
But he was no longer looking down at me

Doloris Ryder
Vincennes, IN

story

push of
sun's tongue
of generosity

in the fit
of a wind's
moment

delivers
imperative
of a leaf whisper

that speaks
where answers dance
in embroidered sands

Michael Kirby Smith
Baltimore, MD

Dedicated to Ellen Cosby and her keen intelligence and compassionate heart.

Glistening Stars

Oh, Phoenix of my desire, ascend for me in pits of fire
Till the fiery end does plague our mortal desire
Then, till the end our hearts will rise
Amongst the stars in dead of night
To see the wonders of the light
Through corridors
Now filled
With
Love
and
Love
Will only then
Bring about
The needs of light
To open
Our hearts
With stars' glistening desires
Will finally lay us
Down to rest
Amongst the mortals we will be.

Carol Lynn Swenson
Eustace, TX

Rosh Hashanah

Retaining the loyalty of Torah,
always year by year, we celebrate
this day—we all are its true adorers,
as humans the God solved to create—
Rosh Hashanah. The sunset may presage
some steep storm, or of fate, a fierce hit,
but our folks hoe the God's New Year's message
will bring good luck—we believe in it.

The reality round will be brighter,
though a space sometimes sends anxious flames
In the Book of Life, the God, Wise Writer,
will enter this year anew our names.
Children and grandchildren will delight us—
them, we hope, the God also will bless
Let in our deals there be no fuss, no muss.
and will escort us, the great success.

We will perform all at the seas and earth,
if the spirit of our Faith is strong,
and will clean our souls by penance and tears,
knowing ways to our goals will be long.
We will, by the sweet wine, apples, honey,
meet this year—hope, days will gaily pass.
Let our future be happy, sunny—
drink, my friend, and then fill one more glass!

Leonid Vaysman
Los Angeles, CA

Hello, New Year

I desperately attempt to start my new round with a lovely piece
of amorphous clay which can form something of which I have
always been dreaming.
The sun with a new face looks at me giving me a larruping good
hug embracing my new scheme of 2016.
I must make sure that I also pay close attention to appurtenances
to my goal of life in order to augment the perimeter of my whole
life whose garden is to have totally new ingredients.
Abjuring many of my shortcomings, which can be skewered,
I must reinstate my own way of life, looking for room for
amelioration.
As I need to perform my ablution to turn over a new leaf and I
need to heal my wounded part of my life, I wish thou 2016 to
provide me with a generous portion of analgesic balm.
Stop me from falling into a wordmonger who is likely to fail to
observe the ultimate rule of the universal communications.
Help me keep it in mind that there are so many capillary tubes
in this world through which I compete with others for what I
embrace so hard until I reach the end of my rope.
Wishing to contribute some amaranthine exploits to the world
while sharing many rib-tickling stories with fellow sojourners on
the planet, I warmly welcome the bright New Year and thank
thee for giving me *joie de vivre.*

Andrew K. Ha
Gibbstown, NJ

*As the year is drawing to an end, I take a vow of making a better one next year.
The same holds true in a day, that is, when the day is coming to a close. I wish
to make tomorrow a better day, and when I greet the morning, I swear that I
will make my today a better one. This poem has come into existence based on
this recurring characteristic often attributed to humanity. I would never stop
searching for new possibilities as if I strove to open up a new field in disciplines.*

I Remember

I remember that day...
when he went away
I didn't ask him to stay,
I let him go away.
I remember that night...
And that fight,
And the silent tears.
I remember the fear...
As he yelled,
She yelled back.
I remember her...
She fought for me,
He was drunk.
I remember my silence...
As I went home,
Slept in my bed,
I never told anyone,
But...
I still remember.

Jessica Vollaro
Barrington, RI

Words

I couldn't find you this morning!
I had so much to say.
You are my voice, the way I create,
for without you, there's nothing but lines.
Without a reason, there is no rhyme!
Although you elude me, you're so clever
the way you hide.
You'll never escape me, for you live in
my mind—
Always waiting for that chance to
be heard.
I'll always write, if I can just find
The words

Darrell Heath Sr.
Chappells, SC

Survive Until the Day

Now alone are those left alive
Forced to stay, wander, and thrive
Upon the broken and trodden earth
Changed so much from its once glorious birth
Instincts warn them to survive
Keeping the mind awake and live
Until the final time has come
When the world will become undone
Though crumbling and desolate it may be
Resist the persistent urge to flee
Stand your ground and continue on
For soon, just wait, it won't be long
The revival that was made for us all
Who have been saved from the inevitable fall

Every closer comes the day
When our Savior comes back to say
Rise up and be with Me today!

Kayla Evans
Wayne, MI

In My Backyard

I left Southern Pennsylvania for
Orlando in pursuit of a dream
With open arms Orlando welcomed and accepted me
Then that shocking fatal night in my
backyard ended in screams
A senseless act of hate that will go down in history

In my backyard 49 innocent people were killed
A twist of fate kept me from exploring the city that night
While 27 minutes away a gunman did as he willed
Hate isn't the answer and will never be right

The scene in my backyard breaks my heart
America, it's time to stop the hate
As hate is tearing us apart
Let's go back to what made our Nation so great

Abigail Hucker
Orlando, Fl

The Banner

The men with boots march.
The soldiers march.

At night there are thousands
with their torches at a rally.
One can see their fanatical
hatred lighting the darkness
And the minds of others.

On and on they go, their
anger burning bright and
unquenchable,

spreading the curse of
hatred and misunderstanding.
Time has not erased the signs.
Reason has fled.

Even now, the people carry
the banner in their hearts
and voices.

The people march.

Karen J. Gilliam
White Settlement, TX

How Can I Hate You?

You promised you'd come on Sunday.
I looked forward to seeing you.
We canceled just the week before
so I could attend my daughter's play.

I prepared for your visit during the week.
Finished decorating my newly painted bathroom,
dusted and vacuumed.
All had to be perfect for you.
Then you sent me an e-mail that
your daughter was coming,
and my heart sank.
I knew you would cancel your day with me.
You said you would definitely
be free the next week.
I was angry, and I said I was busy.
To teach you a lesson (or so I thought)
I sent no more e-mails.
For the next two days I anxiously watched
to see your name on my e-mail list,
and on Sunday it was there.
You said *I know you're angry with me*
and hate me at this time.
How can I hate someone who
brings out the best in me in every way?
How can I hate someone who
compliments me over and over again?
How can I hate someone who
I want to love more than anyone in the whole world?
No, not hate. Just disappointment.

Anita Tornow
West Milford, NJ

The Knock on the Door

The knock on the door,
Two uniformed men…
Chests forward, shoulders erect;
Presidential letter not open,
Military bearing quite correct.
We step into the center hall;
This is not a social call.
Somber eyes confirm my fears,
Now unable to stifle the tears.
Your son's bravery in death
Preserves a great principle;
Such courage and sacrifice
Make our nation invincible.
The letter's platitudes come and go,
As the autumn's hued leaves
Give way to the first snow.
My oldest son perished
In a suicide attack
In our undeclared war
On terror in Iraq.
Awake from a recurring nightmare
With an abrupt start,
The presidential principle
Unable to fill my empty heart!

David Kass
Roslyn, NY

Wild Pig/Lost Habitat

Wild pig lives in the brush, and
For some his life doesn't mean much.
But to secretive friends, like the wood fairy and toad,
The pig defends hidden territory without being told.
His haven lies deep within a shroud of wild jungle
Where diminishing habitat is a concern, and a raven's cry
Often warns frogs and river birds of intruders nearby.
His yard is where a partridge or two finds shelter,
Or an abandoned dog left to die, cries under a darkening sky.
Yet hope never wanes in this assembly of friends, and
Life goes on with dignity and without end.
At sunrise, as the wood fairy delicately touches wild flowers,
And the Creator's light reveals dewdrops fallen from sky,
The dog finds food a stranger left behind.
Kindness is not erased within this hidden realm:
Its occupants here are lovingly embraced as
Sunlight moves across the tops of pine trees,
And geese, hiding in marsh grass press forward
And bravely ascend into morning's endless dream.

Gail Logan
Macon, GA

Pieces of a Puzzle

Walk with us, my Savior.
Lead us by Your hand.
Help us feel Your presence
And know you're in command.

We know we're part of a puzzle, Lord,
The bigger picture hidden,
But each and every piece that's drawn
Is cut and shaped in Heaven.

Only You, Lord, know
How each piece fits together.
For it is by Your own words
That each piece even matters.

So help us, Lord, this very day
To be at one with You
So those just watching closely
Might feel Your presence, too.

Let them know Your love, Lord.
Help us share your gift,
So not one piece of the puzzle's lost
And every life will fit.

Sylvia Lemmond
Highland, CA

Cochise (In Memory)

Throughout our life, God sends us blessings,
And if we're fortunate, a friend of a rare kind.
Such were you, my little white German Shepherd pup,
That came to be a special joy of mine.

Because you had the beauty of a wolf,
Because of my love for the Native Americans and their way,
And you looked so noble, I called you Cochise,
In honor of a great Apache chief of yesterday.

I loved your puppy kisses and wagging tail,
Always happy to see me and came running when I'd call.
I remember how frightened you were of thunder storms,
And how you ran to me until all was calm.

The years have passed too quickly, about 12 in all,
Since I raised you from that little furry pup.
So many sweet memories I now recall,
But never thought of the time I'd have to give you up.

I've seen the pain in your eyes when you try to get up.
But how can I say goodbye to one I love so?
It breaks my heart and I cry for my old pup,
Because it's so hard to let you go.

God's Word tells us about animals in spiritual bodies,
So, now you don't have to suffer and can run free.
But when my life here is over and my spirit returns to God,
I think you will be there waiting just for me…

Frances Atkinson Vaughn
Blanch, NC

Playing Chess

There's no betta place to be
Than playing chess with me.
It all began twenty-four years ago.
At that time, who was to know
together we'd grow...
Small Texas towns and farmland trailers,
I knew you were special
when we first met.
I saw you in a crowd and then you walked
toward the books in a church store.
I followed you... with time on my hands,
saw you pick feminist books off shelves
that caught my eye.
I keep that subject to myself,
but you were special.
To my surprise,
visiting you opened a new
molecule in my heart.
Seeing your cat was almost human —
caring, rubbing her nose
on my ankle, touching my heart —
I wished I had a Rose!
Kitty lies on her bed
like a sensuous teddy bear
Protecting her space.
What was there to fear?
She snuggles up to kitty
wishing it was me...

Alyx Jen
Dallas, TX

Writing poetry and traveling alone in Europe inspired the creative mind for May Sarton's book Solitude. *Creative minds focus during silent periods, which can include meditation. When it inspires others, I thank God for those moments. The World Poetry Movement gave me three gold pins inscribed Best Poet 2012 and a framed certificate for my wall. My book* Baby of the Family *has been published; it describes how growing up playing tennis gave me strength to travel alone to Europe. My silky, long, black hair worn down to my waist drew French men to pick me up at the Louvre Museum. This is the life of a poet...*

drive

life is not always a crisp october morning,
where the asphalt road is clear for miles,
through hues of thinning autumn leaves.
in reality, life is a foggy summer morning in july.
heat rises off the rivers, revealing only
a hundred yards of visibility between you
and everything that lies beyond.
advisors speak of plans, that one should
have a roadmap of where they are going —
a mastermind plan, a landmark, the ideal.
however, life is not a perfect vacation.
it does not come prewrapped
with a beautiful sunset to end each day,
a compass that always points north
or is even right, for that matter.
the truth is, life is scary.
sometimes you need a guardrail
or a street light to guide you.
each individual is just a headlight
on this roadmap without directions,
this challenge tenderly referred to as life,
trying to find their way through every foggy day
with minimal bumps in the road.
the secret is, one can plan, but you cannot
account for every bump in the road or deer in the fog.
sometimes, all you can do is drive.

Alyssa Dawn Betz
Caledoina, MN

Torch

I carry a torch for you lady
Flames arc high
I carry a torch for you lady
Sparks strike the sky
Darling you are the most sincere lady
My life has shown
Love burns in my heart
To you I belong
Magic moments we are united
Blaze my mind
Your radiant beauty
Brands life times
I carry a torch for you, lady
Olympic serenade
I carry a torch for you, lady
Liberty Day Parade
When we embrace
Love starts to warm
To heated undulations
Intense as the sun
I carry a torch for you, lady
Flare bright
I carry a torch for you, baby
Dawn through night
Sugar you will always be
My true love endlessly

Myles Wallace
Chicago, IL

The Attic Space

Happy—just a word, just a thing I
Watch pass like a parade
Of skeletons,
Just a term I've scrapped; and dropped at
The entryway to the little room above my
Place I stay, a crawl space running through the middle,
Boxes piled, half-lopsided; some contents spilling
Out into the light of my hall
A splayed book of pictures, first
Two smiling faces, then five—a swing-set,
Sun, snowy hills and faces red; a
Crying boy with gloves dangling from
Tiny hands with fingers wet and red
From cold; from snowball, from playing out too long
In white, damp weather
And molding snow houses beneath a grey sky
Where more clay falls, and sets:
The image of a little face I can't unsee—the frozen image of a
Near-woman girl who would be killed in 3-2-
All borrowed sadness that was never mine, yet given
As a prize and testament—to a life I have
To lead: to a life not stolen by premature breath, or premature
Death—to a life I am allowed to lead

Joli Schumaker
Rensselaer, NY

To Possess a Poem

To possess a poem you must give as you take.
It invites you to come along.
Some poems need to be whispered or shouted;
Some need to be played like a song.
A poem doesn't need to say just what it means.
It suggests, it reflects, lets you peek at the scene.
A poem leads you to a place you've never been—
Stops and twirls you around,
Lets you look through leaded glass windows
Of beautiful sound
Will you take the risk, step through the mirror?
Something true comes nearer and nearer.
Some poems pinch you and hurt you,
Make you ache and want to cry.
Some poems tickle, they stroke and they poke you,
Make you giggle out loud, and you wonder why.
Words sing in your ears, dance in your space,
Suddenly everything falls into place.
For one sharpened instant the picture is whole;
You have something new that you never possessed.
Because one image struck a chord in your soul.
Everything's balanced, the world is at rest.

Jean Wiegand
Fredericksburg, VA

*I write poems to express my feelings about the world around me to reach
out to others who might feel the same.*

Epilogue

Traditionally the Hebrew months
Are referred to in religious order
From Nissan to Adar
The appointed times straightforward

From Passover to Tu B' Av
With Rosh Hashana right after
Then comes the Day of Atonement
On to Purim filled with laughter

There is much to be learned from the Hebrew months
The surface merely scratched
And learning Hebrew has become
Paramount for the plans I've hatched

Nissan Sivan Cheshvan
Shevat Tevet Iyar
Tammuz Elul Kislev
Tishrei Av Adar

The months as they are
Really do not rhyme
Yet written like the verse above
They do but only just this time

Mark Agnew
Shawnee, OK

Without the Teleprompter

Without the teleprompter
The race becomes a one-man affair
Reality is said to be garbage they read
The disabled are ridiculed in public
Babies are thrown out of the roof
Racism is given triumphant significance
The proud are empowered to cause violence
The fallen and their likes are emotionally tortured
The right man lies to fix the wrong man
And no one gets into a groove

Without the teleprompter
Hate trumps love
Opponents become foes
The media are the lowest form of life
Innocence is the product of misstep risks
Facts equate sarcasms
Losses mean fraud
Go-fund-him changes baton to let's-defund-him
Winning becomes dicey
And losing, the cause of everyone

The teleprompter has done its part of the job
But the onlooker thinks the man is who he is: You name it!

Raymond Obeng
Waltham, MA

Sweet Little Michael

My great-grandson came into this world
on October 11, 2012. When his Dad rolled him
out of the delivery room and I saw his
sweet little face with his eyes so bright
and looking around all over the place, I
knew he was a perfect little boy.
  Michael is now two, and he has
learned so much. He got off the bottle
about the age of nine months because he
could drink out of a glass well so he
got his milk that way. He also ate his
food with a fork; this made him the
center of attraction when they went out to eat.
  He helps his mom with the laundry—he
takes the clothes out of the dryer and puts them
in the basket so she can fold them up.
  When his mom goes to the doctor,
he goes with her; she gives him a
coloring book with his crayons and
he colors while she talks to the doctor.
  Michael lines up his stuffed animals,
then he gets a book and reads to them.
  If Michael does not like something
you do, he points his finger at you and
says *no*.

Jewell Roper
Cullman, AL

America

Who can say where the time goes?
Once gone from here, there is no turning back.
Nature, all its beauty and wilderness, dies
back into the earth and then spring

brings shoots of grass, a baby crocus,
the young tree. The old tree that has been
here for centuries wonders what is this
"Whatever you desire there you are…"

How do you tell a hungry infant born into
poverty that she will not get the education
of leisure, that capitalism will not favor her, and
that all of the food she will eat will not be
worthy of digestion?

This is America, the land of the free.
Free to step over each other running
for a train to quick get home, to quick
eat, to quick sleep and propagate — only
to return, unlike the sun, to a busy
schedule of work for money.

The sun rises and sets in a natural rhythm.
What has happened to America?
The land of the free — a wasteland?
Where there is white trash, red trash, black trash and
yellow trash — built up so high

on sedatives and narcotics to deaden the reality that is theirs.
While the wealthy few — who feed the government which decisions
to vote for and which against — sit back
and wonder where they will travel next for a spasm of leisure.

Julie Anne Weiss
Delhi, NY

*This poem reflects upon country in this election year. It was written quite a long
time ago, however, and it speaks to the hearts of everyone living here. May God
bless America and bless each one reading the thoughts I have to share.*

World to Ponder

A world without the Lord
Is a world of evil
A world without light
Is a world of darkness
A world without kindness
Is a world without caring
A world without brotherhood
Is a world without kindred spirit
A world without hope
Is a world without promise
A world without the sun
Is a world without sustenance
A world without compassion
Is a world without emotion
A world without passion
Is a world without love
A world without faith
Is a world without God
Hence without the latter
The world is lost

Theodore P. Colterelli
Middletown, NJ

Existentialism

Is eating my life
to the ashes of the bones.
Days by moments,
nights by hours
travel through the galaxy
with the magnetic lantern
made of full moon,
searching for the substance
of my existence.
So many questions with
who, what, why…
enter the rhythm of unceasing heart,
but
with the first signal of dawn
my heart inhales the sound of birds singing
from a heavenly orchestra on the oak tree stage,
and
with that melody of nature
I peacefully follow my dreams.

Elizabeth Plater-Zyberk
Miami, FL

June 17, 2016

That's the day my world was turned upside
down. I lost my husband on that day

he died from cancer. Oh God, he fought and
fought so hard; he wanted to live so badly.

But 9 months later he was gone.
Oh Lord, help me be able to live and survive without him.

I was married 40 years and am so broken inside.

I look outside every day just waiting for him to walk by,
but all my memories are all I have left.

I cry when I get up in the morning.
I cry when I go to bed at night.

So please help me get through this, I ask of you, please.

I am just hurting so badly I don't know what to do.
All I know is I don't know how I will get
through this and survive this world without him.

So show me a sign you love me, and you're
here with me, too,

because I will never forget you and I will
always love you so much, too. You're my love,
my life — I will miss you.

Paula Tvrdik
Waskom, TX

Commitment

Like the little train that said, *I can,*
A spirit moves the heart of man
And says to him, *This cause is right.*
So you must push with all your might
   To make it work!

Like the little train that said, *I did,*
A person moved as his heart bid.
And with commitment firm and true,
He did his job and pushed it through,
   He made it work!

Like the little train that knew he could—
He did the things he knew he should.
So to commitment we must bow
The very best that we know how.
   And really make it work!

Lloyd S. Foote
Tempe, AZ

Unknown Riches

Mr. Gilman looked up as a roughly clad man entered.
The man introduced himself, and into his pocked reached.
He pulled out a stone rough and red.
"Will you cut and polish this stone?" he said.

Mr. Gilman held it under a light and fairly gasped.
"Where did you get this?" he hurriedly asked.
"My father found it one day in Hungary on his farm.
He put it in my bag, where I found it safe from harm.

"It has been lying around where it was brought.
My children play with it, and lose it without thought.
Once a rat dragged it down a hole, and it was gone.
I found it so someone had not stolen my stone.

"One night I dreamed it was a diamond, and worth a lot."
"A red ruby!" Mr. Gilman said, "Great value it's got."
The stone was cut — the world's largest ruby ever found.
The poor man possessed a fortune and became unbound.

God has also given us many a great gift.
Still we go along in life and do not attempt to get a lift.
Yet Christ can save all men from want and despair.
Just accept Jesus; He will remove all sorrow and care.

Virchel E. Wood
Redlands, CA

The Loneliest Time

When is the loneliest time? When you can't go to sleep
or wake without that special person's hand to touch,

or face an empty chair with no one there to share
the toast you've made for years,

or the band begins and no one smiles and says,
"Let's dance. That's our song,"

or when a snapshot focuses on memories
of how good the times used to be,

or when one's without the other,
with no one to answer, "Remember when?"

or when no one scratches that unreachable spot
that itches and won't go away,

or it's New Year's Eve and midnight strikes
without a lover's lips to kiss,

or on Valentine's and no one's there
to smooch and hand a single rose,

or at Mass when no one takes your hand
and whispers, "Peace be with you,"

or you pray, "Welcome... all who have left the world
in your friendship" and you feel your loved one's presence,

or as mourners sing, "... when mortal life shall cease
... amazing grace prevails in joy and peace"?

Bill Cento
West St. Paul, MN

216

Mercy

Come accept God's mercy
while mercy is still free.
  Mercy was bought by Jesus
on the Cross of Calvary.
  But if you reject His mercy,
woe unto thee for this is
what will be.
  Vultures come feed on the
humans, the ones who would
not bow their knees.
  Hear their plea for mercy
after they lived life as they
pleased.
  No love for God is in them,
no sacrifice of self.
  Vultures come feed on the
humans for there is no
mercy left.

Judith A. Stanley
Henderson, KY

Shootings

Shootings, shootings, shootings
They use to be far from home
Now it has changed
No longer do they roam

Every day, it seems
To be worse than it was before
What can we do
To open the door

To open up the door of love
That all might enter in
To love thy neighbor as thy self
With God it is a win

Begin the day with prayer
That all might walk on through
That we might love each other
And help each other too

When nighttime falls
And it is time to shut your eyes
Say a prayer of thanks to God
As in your bed you lie

Kayla Kimball
Blue Earth, MN

I was born in Waupaca, WI. I was married and blessed with three children. I started writing poetry when my husband became very ill and I had to be a 24/7 caregiver. Writing poetry after I would get him in bed each night gave me the chance to think about something else, and it relaxed me so I could go on the next day.

Metamorphosis

Larva foraging
Growing increasingly fat
Burgeoning its girth

Spinning a cocoon
Chrysalis incubation
Metamorphosis

Colorful creature
Striking wings of symmetry
Bonny butterfly

Compound eyes alert
Flitting among the flowers
Antennae sensing

Proboscis sucking
Tasting liqueur never brewed
Buoyant butterfly

Mary A. Gervin
Albany, GA

A Love Letter to My Mother

Mother, you are a dream come true,
You have always taught me truth.
Deprived of you, I am unable to bear good fruit.
The level of your dedication has filled me with great appreciation
And has strengthened my very core, making me inclined to do
   much more.
From when I was a child, you stayed right by my side —
At home, at school, and at play, you were with me every day.
You made such a sacrifice in life
By spending all you had to make things right.
You stood beside me in my days of difficulty.
With tears of hope you still believed there was possibility.
You remained my source of inspiration
In all those times of complete frustration.
You continue to be my knight in shining armor,
Both in good times and thereafter.

You possess that same sweet love
That only comes from up above,
That shines all throughout your life
Creating music to birds in flight.
Your moments of victory
Still remain to us a history.

Thank you for this most memorable day
When I can turn to you and now say,
Thanks again for all you have done —
From this day onward, until the setting of the sun.

Marelina Youlanda James
West Haverstraw, NY

Jesus Christ, His Mission

Jesus Christ, the Man,
Came from Heaven to Earth, this land
With a mission so, please, understand.
And before He got here, He was so in demand.
So now read a little bit more about Jesus if you can.
His mission and assignment was very clear,
And I will tell you what it was and still is right here.
His mission and assignment is you and me.
He came to set the captives free
From death, hellfire, and the grave,
So that we don't have to remain a slave.
To sin it is truth, and about that I won't pretend.
Jesus Christ, His mission was to die on a cross and then
Transition from death, Hell, and the grave,
Go back to Heaven, and through the process
He changed our position.
Jesus Christ on this mission
Saved the world for every man,
Woman, boy, and girl.
And for that alone
He deserves our love, trust, respect, and recognition.
People of this world make your call,
And election sure, so that
When you die in Christ and leave this Earth
You too can and will transition — to Heaven.

Earline Hagwood
Columbus, OH

*My name is Mrs. Earline Hagwood. My husband's name is Robert
Hagwood, a good man. We have been married for twenty-five years. I want
to thank him for his love and support always. I thank my Lord and Savior
Jesus Christ for this gift of poetry that He has given to me to be a blessing
to anyone that will read these poems. I love You, Lord. I give You praise,
honor, and glory always, and thank You for using my gift for Your glory.*

Willow

Willow is the name
Of my very
Special friend;
So truly beautiful
She is.

Always will she
Be with me,
Not only in spirit,
But also
In my heart.

Willow is truly
So special;
She comforts me
All day
And at night.

She sees me
For who I am
And loves me,
As I do her.
And even when she
Is gone,
In my heart
She always will be.

Sharon A. Birmingham
Glen Burnie, MD

Always Inspiring Summer

Sometime in the summer
I'll walk barefoot across grass
Blades between my toes, freshly cut
its scent summer in my nose
It will feel cool like green velvet should

Sometime in the summer
My teeth blueberry blue
My breath strawberry red
I'll try to count the stars, the firefly's blinks

Sometime in the summer
There is no quiet
So many bird songs, cricket strummers, cicada hummers
Motorcycles revving, strollers laughing
Thunder booming, raindrops pattering
Loons lamenting, lakes lapping

Sometime in the summer
I'll dream of you
Those I no longer see in daylight
I'll search the night sky
For a falling star
Telling me you are not so far
You're only a heartbeat away

Laura L. Paulsen
St. Paul, MN

Bumblebee

When the Bumblebee hums zzz
My heart rejoices

The honey-combed rain
waxens and mantles my soul

His spirit lifts me to celestial places
where living waters quench thirstily

When the Bumblebee hums zzz
True Light rejoices

The Gloria Reign
panoplies my soul

His fiery sting
pierces and refines me

The golden rings
herald the King

Oh lift me up to heavenly places
so I can see my Master's face

The Glory Bee lifts me
to hallowed places

Now I see
supernaturally

When the Bumblebee hums zzz

Vicki Gonchoroff
Macomb, MI

The bumblebee represents the third person in the Holy Trinity, the Holy Spirit. Scientifically, the bumblebee should not be able to fly, but by divine design it does. This is dedicated to all God's people who yearn for the Holy Spirit baptism. Come, Holy Spirit, come! I wrote this poetic psalm for Randy Travis to sing in his country gospel twang. Randy Travis, call me! In loving memory of Joy Stevens, January 16 1949–April 4, 2016. Psalm 68:11 The Lord gave the Word: Great was the company of those who published it.

A Child Sees It

Is joy the sound of a morning bird's cheering?
The fleetingly quiet scent in a rose?
The vital buzz of humanity—living and breathing?
Is it more than a feeling?
More than as happy just goes?

Is joy a keen, easy alertness—an insight—
Or a mystically happening aura?
Often contagious, more of spontaneous,
Faint, radiant lights filling, uncontrollably spilling,
Which somehow can't help going unnoticed?

Is it just a sweet love… a child-like faith?
Is joy hope, an inner laughter…
Of smiles for all who exist,
The positivity coming after
Some intuitive gift—contentment?

It's really just simple, so extensively simple, so,
Staring out at us plainly, much like a dimple.
It's all these; it's much more!
All is so good—grandiosely good!
There is so much good in our world.

Roberta K. McCoy
Pueblo, CO

Every writer knows the value of a word or phrase that sparks an idea—an idea that can lead to a story and more…to a revolutionary means of understanding even the smallest detail of life. The "storybook gods" can call you up at any time. Ignoring them is pure downfall to a potential author. The inherent magic of words, the fleeting phrase…that spark has embers that die and have a short-lived combustibility unless that wonder is captured, that phrase of understanding, of erudition is put to paper or set to print for a long life to forge perspective.

A Shadow Whose Name...

Hey, Mister! As you pass by each day
I see you, but you don't look my way.
I'm hidden beneath a shadow whose name
Bears resemblance to poverty and shame.

I'm crying. Can you see my tears?
Do you hear me? Does it fall on deaf ears?
Homeless... what has gone wrong?
My hunger has lasted so long.

Maybe one day you'll look here to see
Another where I used to be.
For what hope can I have today
If you keep looking away?

Debra J. Dickson
Bauxite, AR

Be There Monsters?

Sometimes I awake at night
wondering if I'm having a heart attack.
How would I know,
having never had one?
Breathless and scared,
I look about in the darkness.
Where am I?
I search the corners of the room.
Be there monsters here?
I walk the length of the house,
peering through windows,
behind doors.
In the morning I dress
and head off to work,
wondering what may still
be lurking under the bed.

Jeffrey Beyl
Kenmore, WA

Jeff is a writer, a reader, a jazz guitarist and percussionist, as well as a fly-fisherman, scuba diver, marine naturalist, mountain climber, photographer, husband, and father. He also has a day job, but he keeps that a secret.

Romance by Moonlight

I love you so much, my dear.
So why are we apart?
We are opposing poles on life's magnet,
Pulling and stabbing at my heart.

I love everything about you:
How your eyes sparkle like the night
With a backdrop darker than a midnight sky,
And the stars gleam down ever so bright.

Dear, I long to know more about you
To pursue our hobbies and interests together.
How I long to melt in your arms this very night
And bask in its beauty forever.

But how can I declare I love you
As the gap between us widens?
A wall that keeps us on opposite sides
Where love cannot sound its wondrous siren.

I hope you feel the same as I.
This feels too real to be on just one side.
I ask that you return my love with yours
So our romance will no longer hide.

You feel so real in all my dreams,
I love you with all my heart.
But how can I love you oh so much
If we are apart?

Megan Schanzenbach
Ringwood, NJ

I am entering my junior year of high school. Over the past two years, I have taken two creative writing classes, one of which allowed me to participate in Poetry Out Loud. Although my journey ended at the Bergen Performing Arts Center, I hope to be part of it again next year. When not writing, I enjoy being a part of musicals. I am an International Thespian Society member. This year's production of The Little Mermaid *will be my twentieth musical.*

Capped (Probie Classes)

Anatomy was hard.
I was always on my guard.
I never thought I'd pass
Sitting in that class.
Chemistry was the pits.
Over that I had lots of fits.
Micro was tough;
Father Max made sure we all had enough.
Materia Medica was not for us;
The poor little nurses came by bus.
Nursing Arts and all the procedures,
Poor Mrs. Chase—what a chore.
Now that bandaging—it was an art
We liked and studied with all our heart.
Professional ethics—what not to do—
The teacher will always remember who.
Psychology—was for the birds.
Psychiatry—we learned many hard words.
Chem lab—we really fooled around.
A few experiments could have knocked us down.
This bunch of nurses really caused a fuss.
The teachers I am sure learned to cuss.
Finally, the day came when we knew it was all worthwhile,
The day we heard we had passed our first mile—
The day we were capped.

Rita M. Krieger
Ponte Vedra, FL

I am a retired RN, mother of five boys and one girl, all born within seven years. I am a grandmother to seventeen grandchildren, and I love it. I keep busy, I write stories, poems, and books about my family and my life. I also do water aerobics. I babysit and keep up with my grandchildren's activities, and that really keeps me busy—going to lacrosse, soccer, and basketball games, and dances and concerts. By the way, I am eighty-seven years old and still drive.

We Concurred

From R. Rozhdestvensky
Translated from Russian

We concurred—I and you—together
at some day kept forever in mind.
Words concur so with lips, where we get them,
water so with parched throats coincides.

Like the earth at the winter's blow
may concur with awaited snow,
like the birds concur with the sky,
so concurred we both—you and I.

We concurred still without knowing
of World Evil and Good, and just
then severe common time—fast-going—
has forever concurred with us.

Emil Brainin
Pelham, AL

My Friend Within

My friend within is part of me.
She is the part that sets me free.
This friend within—this friend I know,
she loves to dance, be in the flow.
I feel her aura deep inside
and sense that she is at my side.
The universal thoughts she sows
bring out my aura, help it grow.
She always greets me with a smile.
The smile is pure; there is no guile.
She radiates her inner love
and floats suspended up above.
Bestows her crown that radiates,
one that opens starry gates.
With this gift I now can hear
timeless music of the spheres.
I'll wear this crown of joy and love—
love coming from below, above,
far beyond my inner strife,
strife that is a part of life.
I'll open up the starry gates
and seek the joy and seek my fate.
Those gates will open up my soul,
will set me free, will make me whole.

Diana C. Etheridge
Merrit Island, FL

Because I have had a series of health problems, I began to realize that I had to look deep within to seek the answers that I desire. I tapped my inner being and this poem flowed out. I changed very few words and hastily wrote it down. I read it when I feel the need to keep on track with all the projects that I have going on. And here is another thought. I love to tap dance and to learn the complicated steps, most of which came from Blacks who were no longer slaves, but had no jobs so they traveled down the East Coast entertaining interested people. They brought us the beginning of jazz. I believe the rhythm of my tapping and the jazz music also helps me create poems. (Perhaps the vibrations tap into a part of my brain that I had never developed before.) Yes, I know I will overcome my illnesses so that I can continue to tap into my creative spirit.

Musings

I groan as I get up from my favorite chair and
  remember the girl eagerly springing up to dance!
I glance at my hands so wrinkled and with brown spots
  and remember gently stroking my babies' faces.

Where has she gone, this young, spirited woman
  who loved her husband so deeply
and taught her children so carefully?
  I have to concentrate hard to remember.

And who might know my story? Who would listen?
  We each have history buried deep and unspoken.
The world doesn't stop, *time and tide*, you know.
  With body aching with every move, we are left to think.

I used to be important to my husband, to my children,
  to those I taught about business and service,
the people who attended my seminars and wrote
  letters of praise and commendation. But time rolls on.

I'm caught in the river current, drifting along
  toward the terrible progression of age with its
realization that I don't matter much anymore.
  My friends are in the same boat on the same river.

My faraway child calls frequently out of duty, I guess.
  I'm grateful but hate being a burden to him.
He doesn't want that either, and he worries.
  Is mine just a wasted life, a failure?

A broken spirit, resigned to nothingness.
  What really happened to all that promise?

Jeanne Peters
Bradenton, FL

Madison

Dear Little Madison, sweet as
  can be, walks in the door
  and comes right over to me.

You make me feel special,
  like you are to me;
  I wish I could see you
  more, but that's not meant
  to be.

So in the summer I come over
  to swim; you jump on the
  trampoline like it's a gym.

Then you have ice cream in
  a cone, you get dried off,
  and Mimi has to head home.

My love to Madison
From MiMi

Sandy A. Kint
Orrtanna, PA

American Decay

An erie darkness is sweeping through the land.
A prevailing gloom is now at hand.
Turbulent skies swell and froth with fury.
Frightened, we hide, scream, and scurry.
A field of blood covers and paints the street
While all the while, our mothers weep.

Shadows and images of our youth dying
As Evil among us comes out from hiding.
Demons pose as conquering leaders of men,
Moving through our children, one to another and back again.
This once was a nation of love and honor—
Now, egotistical lambs with a thirst for slaughter.

Our country is so much more than black or white.
It has many colors—some harsh, some bright.
Let's rip away the veil, dark cloak,
Covering this nation today
And expose the great tomorrow and the
Proud American way.

Judy A. Alford
Dunbar, WV

I am Judy Alford, now single and starting over late in life. I love poetry and have long enjoyed creating a poem. I grew up loving Shakespeare. I have two children, Charles and Kimberly, and two grandchildren, Catie and Austin, who have brought me the greatest joy. I love God and county. I love my daughter Lisa, my granddaughter Haleigh, and son Wimpy. My life is overflowing! Thanks, Kim, for all your help.

Retro Seek

I had hoped you'd be there when I was old
To help me greet the day
And walk through all romantic thresholds bold
Where we might dine and sup the proper way.

Some did come that day and knock upon my door,
And I was glad to greet them and hold their hands;
I led them to the parlor where we'd sat before
Raising cups gaily and dining on rich viands.

Today with four-score banners crackling in the wind
I wanted more than just a few nearby friends;
This day I sought old, dear friends whose presence rescinds
All fears and darkness and returns us still
To a deep love that life portends.

Donald R. Eldred
Jacksonville, IL

My contribution to the annual Best Poets of 2016 *comes with the overall purpose of lifting my many, many excellent poems, showing forth a good many, really fine and worthy poetic picks. I'm excited and inspired to write more poems because of the* Best Poets *edition. The faith Eber & Wein holds in our work makes us better poets. Thank you for honoring us by featuring one of our own favorite poems.*

Dawn's Dream

I'd like to run out to meet the dawn
On airy, winged feet
And dance along its golden path
Where Earth and Heaven meet.

Perhaps I'd fashion a lovely gown
From dawn's shimmering, rosy light
Or wear a crown of silver stars
Shaken from the night.

Across the little hills I'd dance
With sunbeams for a guide
Until I'd reached the ends of Earth
And paused along its side.

Borne out on the wings of morning
I would dwell in the realms of light
Where morning reigns ever eternal
Having banished all darkness and night.

Ruth Thorud
Eden Prairie, MN

A Regrettable Choice

Each year marks the sands of time.
A penny for your thoughts is now a dime.
Results of an election may be toasted with wine.
If the right choice is made, voters shall be fine.
Through the years, choices have been good vs. bad.
Some choices are not the finest we've ever had.
And results indeed may be very sad.
Consequences turn out quite insanely mad.
Be careful not to be misled by inappropriate views.
Spreading fear, bullying, and inflammatory speech are clues.
Name calling, discrimination and threats bring blues.
These behaviors don't bring good leadership news.
A candidate may be childish, crafty and tend to deceive,
Distorting important issues with tricky tease,
Being mean spirited, insulting, inciting violence with ease,
Fabricating a self pedestal to please.
Look for a candidate with integrity and a forgiving heart.
Endorsing unity, working together, and a new start.
With a purpose of world and nation healing to impart.
And maturely facing obstacles without melting or falling apart.
So, my dears, what more can I say?
Will your November vote turn out okay
With a bit of pre-pondering today?
Hail there lovable Toto and Dorothy from Kansas way.
Toto would be the perfect leader in these times of fray.
To help keep hatred and agitators at bay!

B. J. Boal
Des Moines, IA

Birds Are a Pleasure

Here at the senior center we all
Watch the birds; we have a ball.
Of course the squirrels come to feed;
They try to eat all the seed.
We chase the squirrels; they eat too much.
One day we threw out some bread and such.
A red squirrel took every piece he sees,
And hid each one in the crotch of the trees.
A big black crow arrived on the scene,
Took every piece of bread, how mean.
We watched this tableau to the end.
Birds come to our feeder; we are their friend.
Hope you all feed the birds this year.
It was a rough time for them, we fear.
We were visited by the cardinal, so red,
And the chickadees with the black head.
The titmouse came to call,
As did the junco so small.
A downy woodpecker came to the suet to eat,
And the sparrows were a joy to meet.
We get a lot of pleasure bird-watching at the center.
The seniors here are their mentor.

Barbara King
Clarksburg, MA

Joys of Summer

Summer is here
Oh joy. It's summer.
Sun shines bright and hot
Sun shines through the day.

The temperature is high
It's a furnace outside
The sweat drips down
The faces of those outside

Cool drinks are no comfort
To the roaring heat outside
Ice cream melts to a puddle
Before it is enjoyed.

Summer is here. The heat is here
Beaches are packed with swimmers
I'm sitting here inside
Waiting for fall to come.

Ann Marie Petrizzo
Hazlet, NJ

Penelope's Song

Odysseus!
You leave the shoreline
of this, your known life,
to sail that wine-dark sea.

Its sharp horizon
draws closer in my dreams
like the sound of your footsteps
approaching my door.

Drumbeats of memories
echo down the ages of your absence.
My loneliness embraces
what you left behind.

My loom weaves deception by day.
The fabric unravels by night.
I leave my window ajar
and share secrets with the moon.

She hears my voice
and grants my wish.

You return in triumph,
throw off your disguise,
lay bare my heart.

We cross the threshold of desire.
The years close behind us.
Time holds its breath.

Elizabeth A. Bernstein
Paradise, CA

Jimmy's Flyer

The clocks are set
The owners on hand
The flyers are ready to take their stand
The air is tense
The excitement is rare
The time to take flight is almost here
There they go! Into the air
Whose will be the first to appear?
You slip downstairs for a bite to eat
Then you're back on the roof to follow the meet
There they come circling low
You shout and holler, *That's my boy*
Your heart is jumping with pride and joy
It is your bird, you can see
And guess what his band reads, *Why it's 583*
There he comes diving down
He looks like he has seen the town
The race is over
The money is paid
Now to the next one
For which they all wait
The pigeons are snuggled all tight in their coops
While the owners are out in some bar spinning loops
The talk that is heard shouldn't be spoken in words
So happy racing to all
And to all a good flight.

Ellen Pess
Massapequa Park, NY

Microburst

A father, a mother, a daughter, a son —
A house with three levels, living room on level one.
Second floor had bedrooms for dad and mom
Third floor had bedrooms for daughter and son.
The day had been rainy with lots of strong wind.
Night came. All slept peacefully, the house within.
A loud clap of thunder startled parents awake.
They went to the hall to investigate.
Sound of a freight train going through living room.
Such a pressure on ears! Their heads might go boom.
Loud crash from upstairs. Children's windows blew in.
Parents rushed upstairs to check on the din.
Whirlwind in motion of toys, shoes and pants —
A neighbor's roof shingles joined in the dance.
Above a carpet of shards of glass —
The spectacle left both parents aghast.
The children slept through all the din.
Whisked to the living room children were then.
Checking them showed they had not a scratch —
A wonderful thing that had not a match.
Destruction in the children's room was the worst;
Like an upside down tornado, the wind had a microburst.
Tornados spin down to up, microbursts up to down.
The difference matters not if it hits your part of town.
Floors can be swept, windows repaired.
Thankfully, the lives of the children were spared.

L. Janeene Versfelt
Raritan, NJ

*My phone rang at 1:30 AM. My son Charles asked, "Mom, are you okay?"
I said, "I'm fine. I was sleeping." He said, "We just got home and our house
is trashed. The three pillars in front of the house are broken. Tree branches
are all over the yard. My next-door neighbor's wheelchair ramp broke into
pieces. Our roof is damaged and our fence is down." He and the family in
the poem had damage to their homes, but no one was hurt.*

A Castle Made of Sand

I was walking down the beach one day
and came upon a special place by the sea.
I will build a sand castle here
That can be seen far and near,
where people can see as they pass by.

I made my castle not far from the sea.
It was a beautiful sight to me.
I made it with my bare hands,
not thinking of the shifting sand.
My thought was where the castle would stand.

I stepped back and looked around.
I gazed with pride, with tears in my eyes.
Oh! Isn't this a sight to see,
sitting by the deep blue sea?
A perfect castle named after me.

I decided to walk down the beach again
And thought how marvelous the castle was.
I will go back and think for a while,
that I am walking down the halls,
looking through each door between the walls.

But the castle wasn't there.
I should have known;
it was made of shifting sand,
too close to the sea where I stand.
God will give me time again.

Jewel A. Durham
Littlefield, TX

Goodbye

Goodbye to waking up each day
To that small park where children play,
The summer heat, winter's cold sting —
Goodbye, goodbye to everything.

The smell of roses, baking bread,
The bee that's buzzing round my head,
To watching sister on the swing —
Goodbye, goodbye to everything.

The sound of silence in a room,
The swishing sound of Mama's broom,
To grandma's old, gold wedding ring —
Goodbye, goodbye to everything.

The howling dog, the noisy cat,
The bench where we would sit and chat,
And old rag doll, a ball of string —
Goodbye, goodbye to everything.

The time you spent all day in bed,
The colors purple, orange, and red,
The fallen bird with broken wing —
Goodbye, goodbye to everything.

The list is endless when you start
Remembering who touched your heart;
That sad song that you loved to sing —
Goodbye, goodbye to everything.

Jo Ann Blunkall
Paonia, CO

Forget

I believe in forgiveness, love, the healing of time,
the importance of family and close friends of mine.
All make mistakes and perfection, an illusion,
but perpetual forgiveness is pure disillusion.

A person who's hurt me again and again —
Whose selfishness keeps taking, never to end —
Who finds sport in kicking me when I'm already down —
And keeping their hand on my head as I drown —
Tears I have spilled on those long, countless nights,
Because I wanted to forgive, just to end the fight.

Forgiveness is noble. Love for all, the goal.
Hatred, blame, grudges… All the time they stole!
But when my arms are held wide open yet again,
I'm insulted, let down and hurting instead.

I can't let it happen, for my own sanity.
It's time to move on. It's time to be free —
Free from the pain that I keep deep inside.
It's self-preservation, not a matter of pride.

I never imagined that I'd think these thoughts.
The truth is so close. I'll tell it… I aught.
So here I am, thinking it, writing it — see?
She may still be alive, but she is dead to me.

Katherine O. Flower
Somerset, NJ

Having Fun with Our Twins

Having twins is where the work, some fun, begins.
Twin girls or twin boys
They are like playing with toys.
They say you inherit the twin genes
So we really know what that means.
Doyle and Don Davis first of all, twin boys,
Then came our two, Glenda and Bobby.
No twins we had, and we were really glad.
But one day the phone rang, our twins are here.
Mark and Mindy Sjolander and they were so sweet and dear.
But wait, a few years later the phone rings again…
We have twin girls, Leslie Ann and Heather Lynn.
Good news, exciting to hear again.
They are all grown up now and fun we do have.
They run, laugh, scream and play,
and ride their scooters most of the day.
They like to spend the night and sleep with me.
So I try to make them feel safe and secure.
They are intelligent and smart,
They say, "Memaw, rub our backs, sing into my heart."
So they slip away into sleepy land and rest all night —
But always ready for breakfast at first daylight.
So if you have twins, enjoy them all you can.
They'll soon be grown up, out of your hands.
I love all my twins.

Lucille Tyler
Liberty, TX

There'll Always Be an England

We've traveled all over Europe,
(and this makes our 6th time)
  So we though it right to put all
our memories to rhyme.
  Germany, France, and Italy
were fabulous to see,
  But in all the world there's just
one place for these travelers to be.
  Oh! To be in England, when the
flower gardens bloom,
  And the royal guards at Buckingham
do make the ladies swoon!
  The grandeur of the castles
and the booming of Big Ben
  Can make the weary traveler want
to *Haste ye back again*
  From the thatched cottages of the
Costwolds to the White Cliffs of Dover,
  It's like the *singing of the Sirens*
That calls you, *Come back over*
  The Romans stayed 300 years to
conquer this great land,
  And they left the city of Londonium,
as their armies did disband.
  There's so much to see and do here,
as one travels to and fro.
  And the London fogs seem to
whisper, *Dear friends, do not go*.
  Well, I've rambled on enough, and
the time it steadily goes.
  So, God bless you, British cousins,
and God keep you, *English Rose*.

Norm Smith
Columbus, OH

The UN Is Sleeping

The UN is sleeping
While mothers are weeping
Young men are being slaughtered
While playing their game
The UN is sleeping
and has no shame
Young girls are being captured
And sold worldwide
The UN is sleeping
Has its face to hide
The UN must assemble an army
Made up of its member states
and destroy all of ISIS
Before it's too late
and if it doesn't act soon
And destroy what we face
It will wake up one morning
And find itself at the stake

Samuel Lombardo
Destin, FL

From Fort Fisher to the Titanic

One of the shining stars of the Confederacy during the American Civil War was Thomas Pondford.

He got his start by making improvements to Fort Fisher near Wilmington, North Carolina.

These innovative improvements kept the fort in Confederate hands until 1865. He was a deeply religious man.
Thomas attended the same church President Jefferson Davis did.
He praised Jesus Christ with his words, money, and deeds.

After the Civil War's end, Pondford became an ordained minister.

He served Jesus with passionate speeches of fire and brimstone.

Thomas distinguished himself by designing improvements to harbors and ocean liners.

His last assignment was as chaplain on the Titanic. He died in the iceberg disaster, and he praised Jesus with his dying words.

Tom Burkacki
Hamtramck, MI

The Wall

Slowly, hesitantly,
I think of a wall
closing me in.
Trying not to fall,
walking closer to
a window of ancient themes
and forgotten dreams.

Looking through the window,
I see a brick wall,
and I hear the call
of an ocean tide,
rushing in
and rushing out,
roaring on the other side.

Tony Tripodi
Jacksonville, FL

Intruder

A tribute to the victims of the Pulse Night Club, Orlando, FL

Gale winds create dark waters drowning the spirit within his soul!
Now forming torrential rains of forbidden retribution! A strong
snap and crackle of earth's winds flame and stoke the fires of hate!

The rustling of leaves awakens a dance with all-consuming
despair! Molten lava drips a slow, black death. A tremor shakes
the grounds a twist of fate of who will be found! Destinies are
sealed with a kiss! Neglect can create the perfect storm! Weather
has no conscious either, with random acts of no remorse!

A cruel shaken reality rips people apart! Like nature's prey with an
un-forgiving solitude. Leaving the innocent to pick up the guilt!

Victoria A. Josephson
Melbourne, FL

Flight of the Hawk

As I tread the concrete sidewalk
This Mother's Day in May,
I'm reminded of your mother,
My sister, Ilise,
How she died suddenly without warning
And how you died a year later
Of a broken heart.
I pause on the sidewalk
And stare up at a hawk
Spiraling over a grove of aspen
Just starting to leaf out.
The hawk circles,
Then wheels away to the west.
Goodbye, Brandon,
The flight of the hawk.

Richard Stepsay
Aurora, CO

Bullets

Do bullets ever fall to the ground?
You know, the ones shot into the air.

Do they travel on as to cascade the sky.
Where angels assigned to catch them care,
like Tinker to Ebers to Chance, them Cubs!

I wonder where do bullets fall,
the ones so carelessly aimed to the sky,
on buildings short and tall they fall.

I wonder about those many things,
carelessly aimed to the sky with ease.
Falling on someone's vintage cars,
or rooftops where some pigeons live.

Where angels assigned to catch them care,
like Ruth, Mickey, Roberto C. and Shoeless Joe,
with wings on his feet.

Steve Arlington King
Brooklyn, NY

This poem was inspired by the film The Mexican, *featuring Brad Pitt, Julia Roberts, and the late James Gandolfini.*

Summer Rain Storm

It fell from sky to earth
and all it touched smelled sweet
gave life back to the parched dry soil
that had given up in sleep
Drenched the leaves on all the trees
and swept across the land
and I could see from far away
the visual sight was grand

Billowy
dark clouds
at their bottom
were long dark sheets
way off in the distant sky
great long lightning streaks
Thunder roared
pierced the air waves
through

the wind picked up
blew about
very
ominously
too

I looked on in wonder
as anyone would do
hoping that before day's end

I'd feel the shower too

Charlotte Neukam
Redondo Beach, CA

Always Right and Never Wrong

Up and down and all around,
forward and backwards, a beautiful smile and an ugly frown.
You never know what each new day will bring or will take away.
Will we benefit or will we pay?
It would be wonderful to win each day, but life does not always
   let us choose
who will win or who will lose.
Just try to sing a happy song—day or night, black or white,
sun up or sundown, from dusk till dawn, dark or light, wrong
   or right.
Hot or cold, the young or the old,
the green leaves on the trees or the brown ones on the ground.
Right in front of you or hiding in plain sight,
standing behind you or to your left or your right.
Clear blue sky or full of dark clouds,
sun-shiney day or rain pouring down.
Coming and going on your life's journey takes you down your
   own road.
Is it straight and narrow or full of curves, bumps, and stones?
Quiet or noisy, hard or soft, sweet or sour, salty or bland,
boy or girl, woman or man.
Are your tears for happiness or are they sad?
Life is full of both the good and the bad.
But do not give up, just take a stand!
God said just ask me and I will give you My helping hand.
Have faith, hope, and love in God above.
Always thank God for everything.
Never blame Him for anything.
He is always right and never wrong!

Deborah S. McNease
Leesburg, GA

One Thought

One thought, strongly held, will lead some to life,
Though it brings to their roadways boulders and strife.
A gauntlet is entered — so many opposed —
Voices berate, but the right path it shows.

One thought will anchor some amid masses that spew,
There's safety in numbers! Why go with the few?
Men rise up and claim that their way will endure.
They teach what is easy. God tells what is sure.

One thought will guard some, as the centuries change form;
Unlikely to most (yet, really the norm).
A lone number holds sway here (a thought that's not new):
By one man keep living… Jehovah is who.

Wayne Mitchell
Red Oak, TX

Our Phoenix Shall Rise Yet

While somewhere in the mind our demons hold the reigns
While somewhere in the mind we're moving at their will
While somewhere our feet are taking us to nowhere
To nowhere on the old treadmill

While somewhere in the heart our tears are being wept
While somewhere in the heart we're yearning for someplace
While somewhere our souls are mourning all the no ones
The prisoners lost along this race

Yet somewhere in the mind our freedom rings
Yet somewhere in the heart our dreams reside
'Tis here new hope unfolds her lovely wings
And spreads them far and spreads them wide
'Tis here new songs the troubled spirit sings
Those songs our former selves denied
'Tis here new life from ancient ruin springs
As pure now as a virgin bride

Oh 'tis somewhere, somewhere
'Tis somewhere, someplace
'Tis somewhere, somewhere
'Tis somewhere, someplace
Our phoenix shall rise yet
With glorious grace

Lisa G. Manning
Gloucester, MA

While this poem was initially written purely about myself, it soon developed into one about humanity in general. We as a people have lost our way. I cannot believe that human beings are intended to wage war against each other, pollute the environment, abuse creation, enslave their minds to technology, or worship fame and fortune. Though in my heart I may be weeping for all of us, there too, buried deep within me, lies the hope that somewhere, someplace, our freedom is still ringing, our dreams are still residing, and that somewhere, sometime, we shall walk tall once again.

My Perfumed Love

My love, among the most
    perfumed flowers you are.
My soul beats with a celestial
music that guides me to you.
All my body dances internally
    when I approach you.
Intense love never felt for you,
I feel like a part of Heaven
covers us as if it was
    ours alone,
love never felt between two
human beings, creation
of God.
Bless the creator for
    creating souls that love
    as I love you.
You were created for me —
perfumed love reactivates
    my life when you
    approach me.

Claro C. Feliciano
Culebra, PR

*Dear friends, I am eighty-three years old. My father was a poet
and my oldest sister also. So I have inherited being a poet and will
continue writing many more poems. God bless you.*

Gone Are the Days

From out of the blue I am coming to you.
I will simply take you by the hand,
And I hope you will finally understand
The dire emergency throughout this land.

America is not now what it was meant to be.
We must open our eyes and then we will see.
The good Lord had this magnificent plan
For all to share in this enchanted land.

When once again we are free, America then will be
The land that we love with the good Lord again above.

This was the plan from Heaven above:
Where all nations would live in peace and love.
Why must all other countries continue to fight and die?
Why can't we find peace for you and I?

The rest of the nations now laugh at you and me.
They think we are ignorant and cannot see
The urgency spreading across our homeland.
There is no longer love for our fellow man.

When once again we are free, America then will be
The land that we love with the good Lord again above.

Ruth Takano Sliger
Amarillo, TX

The Leprechaun

I awoke this morning at six
And thought my eyes were playing tricks
For there up on a little shelf
Was the cutest little elf
Dancing all by himself
Singing low an Irish ditty
Which I thought was very witty
Twinkling bells were on his toes
He was wearing Kelly Green Clothes!
When he saw that him I spied
He turned around, tried to hide!
Then looked at me and slowly smiled
Beaming like a mischievous child!
This must be a silly dream
On some crazy mixed-up scheme!
What are you doing here this morn?
And are you really a Leprechaun?
You may think that I am dumb
But tell me where did you come from?
This very colorful little rogue
Answered with an Irish brogue
I came from the land of sun
And I came here to have some fun!
Making hearts merry and gay
For today is St. Patrick's day!

Antoinette Italiano
Middletown, NY

In the Name of Chance

All prim and proper, super clean cut
Walking like peacocks with a strut
To win growing in their gut
If they don't, they sneer and pout

The rustling of the bingo cards
Like leaves on a birch tree
Hoping for glory and rewards
Winners they hope to be

The night half gone, changing callers
Tired one exits, new one sits in
If a mistake is made, one hollers
Now! That's a mortal sin

Specs halfway down their noses
Like lions waiting for their prey
Or leopards at their poses
Here I am again I guess I'll stay

Another night comes to an end
I hurry up gather my gear
To the losers, my ear, I lend
Ah! But at least I enjoyed my beer!

Florence Richmond
Wauconda, IL

Welcome Home

Our world seems to be smaller, but really, it's the same
   we just need to alter thoughts — re-program our brain
broaden understanding, perceive the point of view
   our brave new populace has hopes and dreams like me and you

They live their days with purpose, have goals they will pursue
   and bring with them their own perspective — how to continue
With diligence and fortitude they each have gifts they share
   our refugees have come to us for shelter — hearts that care

Do we embrace the words hailed by our Lady Liberty?
   "Give me your tired, your poor,
   Your huddled masses yearning to breathe free,
   The wretched refuse of your teeming shores.
   Send these homeless, tempest tossed to me.
   I lift my lamp beside the golden door."°

Again, I ask, do we reflect the image she projects
   accepting them with open arms that they've come to expect?
Do we live the words we utter nobly, speaking love and peace
   and not just empty words, but "Welcome Home" where fears and
      hatred cease?

Pat Evan
Austin, TX

°*Emma Lazarus*

Nobody Knows

My name? What are you saying?
That's not my name!
You say you are drawing a blank?
Have no regret. I frequently fret
That nobody knows my name!

The bill collector knows where I reside.
My address suffices. No surprises!
My name? I hate it!
But I'd love to hear you say it, my name!
Warning: Do not call me, if you don't know.
Hey, you or *You with the blond hair.*
You won't know, I fear!
So I'll pretend I can't hear!

Just then, someone called Maria.
Why not me? But I like it, the name.
I'll go see. First I would say:
"My name's not Maria."
And what is it, your name? I'd like to know!
My name is, shall I say it? My name is….. Joe!
As in Josephine: Joe!
A long pause: *You're nobody I know!*
A girl with the name Joe?
Back to business: I was just singing a song. Or was I?
I must have spoken the name Maria.
I can't remember, so I'll just ask Joe. She'll know.

Laverne Foltz
Tucson, AZ

Historic Salem

Entering Salem you will see
The church and steeple established by Jason Lee,
Who entered Oregon's Willamette River Valley
To teach the Indians spirituality.
The spire stands straight and tall,
Visible to all.
It commands your view of the sky
And is revered by all passing by,
Held in a deep respect of wonder and love,
Shared with the Lord above.
What a beautiful and emotional sight to see —
This wondrous steeple peeking through the trees.

Julia Hittle
Keizer, OR

I Repent

Lord, I am shackled by my guilt
I wear a heavy coat of shame
I've lost my moral compass
With no one but myself to blame

Father, I fell into the world's evil ways
Whatever suited body and mind
Doing all sorts of indecent things
Walking in darkness, completely blind

Many times I've been a loser
It was difficult to win
Satan, got his grip on me
Dragged me down road of sin

Open my lips, O God
My mouth will declare Your praise
Renew the Holy Spirit within me
Love and forgive me, all my days

All I want is to know my Savior
To experience His resurrection power
Share His love and suffering
See the face of Jesus, my final hour

Lord, you have showered me with blessings
My life will never be the same
I give You thanks, praise, and glory
And I bless Your holy name

Amen

Franke Hildreth
Zephyrhills, FL

yellow brick logic

consider the man
made of tin
search for heart
where to begin

why did scarecrow
need a brain
talk about going
against the grain

lion caused commotion
when confronted withdrew
courage was lacking
might trouble ensue

dorothy and toto
wanted back home
all set off
to wizard's throne

emerald city moral
wish granting forgo
self-reliance own reward
confidence will bestow

Marc Miceli
Nalcrest, FL

Sorry, I Can't Hear You

Rise and shine
Daughter dear
Said a voice from afar
Sorry, I can't hear you

Make your bed
Clean your room
Said a voice from afar
Sorry, I can't hear you

Take a fruit
With your lunch
Said a voice from afar
Sorry, I can't hear you

Homework done?
Please say yes!
Said a voice from afar
Sorry, I can't hear you

Call me please
After three
Said a voice from afar
Sorry, I can't hear you

Need some cash
Mother dear
Said a voice from afar
Sorry, I can't hear you

Ireneanne Novell
Palm Beach, FL

The School Christmas Play

The children's faces were happy
At the school Christmas play.
They clapped and sang so gleefully
At thoughts of their holiday.

"Frosty the Snowman" and "Rudolph"
And "Jingle Bells" so gay,
But not a word about Jesus
At the school Christmas play.

No mention of any angels
Singing sweetly at His birth;
The star so brightly above Him—
A guide to all the earth.

"'Tis Jesus Christ our Savior's birth!"
I wanted to rise and say.
But no word of Him was spoken
At the school Christmas play.

When I was a child so long ago
Went to the school Christmas play,
We sang "Away in a Manger,"
Of Him sleeping on the hay.

"Oh, Little Town of Bethlehem,
How still we see thee lay."
We knew just what was celebrated
At the school Christmas play.

It warmed our hearts to learn of Him.
And everyone would say
With happy faces all aglow,
What a fine school Christmas play!

Ruth G. Ray
Macon, GA

Windows to the Soul

Look at us; don't turn away. Look into our eyes.
They are the windows to the soul. If you really
listen to us, you will see that we are like everyone
else, just like you inside. We laugh, we cry, we hurt —
we hurt more than others because everyone sees
us differently, but in God's eyes, all children are
God's children. We hurt, but we come right back,
and even if we are different, we are here for a
purpose. That purpose we don't know yet, but God
knows, and He will let us know. Don't turn away
because it is as if you were turning away from God.
God made us in His image and we all came from dust
and to dust we will return. God loves you and
so do we, so don't reject us, look into our eyes,
which are the windows to the soul!

Angelita Chapa
Robstown, TX

I am seventy-four years old. I married the love of my life. It's so sad now; he's been gone three years. He passed February 22, 2013. We had two beautiful daughters, Annette and Melinda. Annette, our firstborn, was born with a disability and suffered much rejection. She was the inspiration for this poem.

The Cycle of Love (Life)

For my children

I was sitting here thinking, back when you were small,
A freshness of your baby smell; you looked like a Barbie doll.
But then something happened, you changed.

I turned around and you were grown, grabbing at society's world,
Now you're on your own.
The cycle of life has come around one more time,
The cycle of life will continue forevermore, the cycle of life will
   always keep score.

I still picture those treasured thoughts. My inner movies I keep
   and save.
Memories that I can always relive—that, I'll take to my grave.

But time has slipped away; you've gone with little or no fear.
But always remember this: if you reach out your hand, I'll be near
   or there.

The cycle of life, a chain that will not break.
The cycle of life, a promise made in Heaven.
The cycle of love—made by woman and man.

Still sitting here thinking,
Back when you were small.
Now that you're truly no longer here, I ask this:
Please, don't forget to call.

James Edward Horton
Sutherlin, OR

Kindness

Kind is the sky and the wind. Beautiful and soft.

Kind are those who have love in their hearts for those
whose lives touch their own.

Although the world is filled with strife and evil, goodness
and kindness can prevail.

But people desperately need to be reminded to love God
and others as He has loved us. Indeed, kindness may well save the
world.

Kind — such a small, little word that brings to mind
quietness, gentleness, respect, and compassion.

No wars, no hate, no murder, no children going hungry —
sounds like Heaven.

Everyday kindness can have a ripple effect, floating like a flock of
beautiful exotic butterflies over the earth.

Why not? It is up to you and me — the ordinary people — we
have the power! By God's grace. Everything we pray for the
world to be is within our grasp.

So I ask: Are *you* ready to be kind? Are *you* willing to be kind?
Are *you* willing to change the world? What a wonderful goal to
work toward every day.

I put my hand in yours and what we could never do alone, we can
accomplish together!

Shirley A. Westbury
Richmond, VA

*I want to acknowledge Dr. Daisy Reed, retired professor of English at Virginia
Commonwealth University for her continuing support and her request of me to
write a poem on kindness.*

It's Christmastime

The calendar has turned, now it's December.
　Many happy moments are ours to remember.
The family will gather; it's Christmas once more.
　There are presents to buy, time to head to the store.
One day I couldn't find you; you were quiet as a mouse.
　You were outside, putting lights on the house.
You came to find me; you had something to show.
　I couldn't believe it; the house was all aglow.
Get out the decorations, put up the tree.
　Hang the lights and bells; it's so beautiful to see.
Find the ornaments; we love each one.
　The tree will really sparkle when we are done.
We both love Christmas, a special time of the year.
　Gather the family; it's great to have them near.
The stockings are hung, cookies are in the oven.
　A kiss under the mistletoe, we share some lovin'.
It's been snowing; it snowed all through the night.
　The air is crisp and cold; it's a beautiful sight.
I decorate the table, lay out the dishes.
　Soon we will all gather, full of holiday wishes.
A knock on the door, our family is here.
　Get out the nog, add a little cheer.
We're here together again, so much laughter.
　These are times we will remember forever after.

Janice Smith
Harrisonville, MO

My husband died four years ago. While preparing for Christmas last year, I wrote this poem. It's about past Christmases and happier times. It's hard to think about Christmas without thinking about him. Christmas was his favorite time of year. When a loved one dies, it takes time to move on without them. The best thing you have are your memories and wonderful times like these—times when you are surrounded by family and friends.

The Red Ball

The red ball rolled toward the staircase
And then it bounced
  Down a step,
    Down a step,
      Down a step,
Then down several more steps
Until it came to the floor
And began to roll once more.

A smile appeared on the child's face
As his gaze pounced
  Down and then
    Down and then
      Down and then
Down again, his mouth all grins.
So he could watch it once more
He retrieved it from the floor.

Robert P. Tucker
Lakeland, FL

In today's world with all of its disturbing news, I am always happily reminded by my grandsons Jack and Tom (now five and three) of one of life's great joys and pleasures: just being a grandparent, watching and playing with one's grandchildren. Out of such experiences I have been moved to write several poems including "The Red Ball."

Young to Old

When you are young and get to grow old,
you can do things at first and be bold.

As time goes by and you change,
your life is good and has no range.

You think clear thoughts with room to spare;
your body is strong and you have hair.

Don't be too hard on yourself today;
The Lord is with you all the way.

You may not run or jump or skip.
That's okay, just drink your coffee with a sip.

Your life is good, though you've lost some friends,
you make new ones around life's bends.

You learn to enjoy the little things,
putting on pants and driving in your lanes.

Remember the things you used to do;
just laugh out loud and don't be blue.

Gretchen A. Dunham
Nashville, IN

I enjoy writing poems in this world of stress. It helps me realize I'm not too sad.

Everly

It won't be but a blink
When we see a little girl in pink
Granddaddy and I can't wait to see
The little girl given by God with glee
May God bless her every day

Mom and dad will be so proud
When she arrives and her cry is loud
They will beam from ear to ear
Because their baby, Everly, is finally here
May God bless her every day

Won't Eli be glad when sister arrives
He will be a great help as she thrives
They will love each other
As does every sister and big brother
May God bless her every day

Grandmeme will be there to take
The first opportunity to hold her namesake
Uncle Blake will arrive in a nonchalant way
Hoping someday her heart his way will sway
May God bless her every day

Peggy S. Collier
Canyon, TX

The Squirrel

Sitting at lunch in the cooling breeze
A frisky squirrel scampers
Where else but Florida in November
Can I rest myself and pamper?
The squirrel hunts and searches the grass
He's content 'cause he knows he's safe
His children are here; his cousins too
He's secure not knowing his fate
I know he's a rodent but feel no fear
I wonder what he is feeling
He flicks his tail then turns around
His actions make him appealing
He studies me, who might I be?
He sniffs as he looks me over
I offer him scraps; they're all I've got
He glances over his shoulder
I offer him my apple core
What's left of my now-eaten lunch
He considers it, then runs off
To seek a more generous bunch!
I'd like to reach out and stroke his head
To let him know he's cute
Tomorrow I'll bring him peanuts to eat
And not leftover fruit

Denise Hengeli
Plantation, FL

The Passage of Maringo

A warm winter day down by the bay.
Major Maringo basked away.
As if by command, he arose from the sand.
And sped to the sea with surfboard in hand.
Next thing he knew the board split in two.
Major Maringo was lost from view,
His body absorbed by the force of the tide.
He became nimble as a feather in the wind.
His mind emptied of all pain and joy.
He rendered his fate to the ocean.
Time stood still; as an electric drill,
He bore head first into the ocean floor.
The impact was enough to shatter his face,
Instead he burst into space
To escape the ocean depth,
To a pendency was impossible.
Yet the major was there suspended in air.
A bolt, a sudden jolt sent the major in a spiral.
The twirling subdued to the reality of icy smooth marble.
Maringo rubbed his throbbing head.
He tried to adjust his vision, but the darkness was total.
The cold floor and the blackness made his damp body shiver.
He stood for an eternity frozen with fear.
Questions and answers raced through his mind.
He could not rationalize or even fantasize.
He advanced step by cautious step with trembling arms
Waving into the obscurity before him.
Each wary footstep brought forth a feeling of dropping
To the edge of the universe plunging into oblivion.
In Quadrant H Sector 5, a body was found barely alive.
To this day none can say Major Maringo has passed away.

Mark Franko
Hutchinson, KS

So It Doesn't Hurt

I need you here with me
So it doesn't hurt
Come be with me
Seeing the outline of your face
Your smile off from a distance
Your hands so close, so strong
As we walk hand in hand
Be as one
Our voices of sweet melody
We can dance the night among the stars
I need you here, so it doesn't hurt
To savor our love with the bliss of our souls
Till now, till forever

Dorothy Ann McFarlane
Maynard, MA

Lonely

To bed at 11:00 PM, up at 7:00 AM,
The wind is blowing and the sun is bright.
Another day and another night.
My days are long and my nights are short.

I've always worked and been busy all my life.
Looked forward to retirement but found its not that nice.
Raised five children and been married twice.
But now retired and I just don't what to do.

Clean my house and my yard too.
Try to stay busy but again its not easy.
Walk the dogs, feed the cats.
Sweep the porch do this and that.

Now I know how lonely you can get.
Have a few friends but don't know where they are!
Family lives out of state, but they have their own lives too.
So I'm selling my house to get close to them.
And I will make sure they will know where I am!

I've told my story and as far as I know
I've lived a good life and this is so.

Neva Rootes
Largo, FL

Poet Tree in Motion

In desperation, I sought high and low for a magical
    kind of tree
Where wind-blown rustling leaves fling away with
    swing and sway incessantly
Awesome, gigantic sprawling limbs reach out their
    leafy fingers just as graceful as can be
Perhaps that's why it's affectionately thought of
    as the poet tree
I'd searched far and wide as far as eye can see
Till finally, my hand snagged one twirling leaf
    spiraling downward from that poet tree
Then suddenly, miraculously, and unexpectedly, my
    reinvigorated fountain-pen began swirling out
    grandiose words of pure ecstasy
Some say, there's really no such thing as a
    "poet tree"
All I can say is, "Look inside of your own creative
    self, there you may find another twirling
    leaf about to be"

William H. Shuttleworth
Jacksonville, FL

*This poem came together for me during all the falderal through the election season.
For me, writing poetry (at times) serves as an escape to Utopia. There in solitude,
I can sort out my complexity of thoughts and emotions and then reconstruct
into a creative expression of art. I'm so glad that God remains securely on His
throne and "holds the whole world in His hands." A consoling Bible verse for me is
"Casting all your care upon Him; for He careth for you" (1 Peter 5:7).*

last day (for Charlene)

funeral today.
as usher, I touched the white linen cloth
w/ embroidered scarlet cross draped over the casket
and seemed instantly transported inside w/ the body.

then loaded into the hearse
and the long, long ride
to the canopy-covered gaping hole.
prayers, some tears — a few openly weeping.
I began to feel a bit sorry for myself,
but mostly for the pain I caused mourners.

then down and down into the pit,
followed by a gentle thump — a fitting
conclusion to my surrogate death.

some final nose-blowing, receding footsteps,
then soft susurration of sand on casket cover.

how, I wondered, was I still breathing?

oh, yes, as usher I'd lit the candles for service —
now snuffing them, smoke curling high
and higher to the wooden cross hanging above.

only then could I grieve.

Joseph H. Kempf
Indianapolis, IN

His Legacy

If he crossed your path
He showed you love
And told you about Jesus
And Heaven above
Home at last, he now can say
No more sorrow, no more pain
He loved his family
And his friends
Stay true to Jesus
And we will meet again
This is what I believe he would say
Just one last word about getting saved

Judy Pannell Moon
Vinemont, AL

In loving memory of my husband Rev. Billy Moon: April 5, 1950 – May 9, 2016.

Mankind

Life is deep—like an ocean—
A place to soak your feet,
Indulging yourself
In the world that surrounds you.
Forever searching the depths of ourselves,
Constantly contemplating—
Asking all the *whys* and *what ifs*.
But also to never be satisfied
Because satisfaction is merely mediocre,
And cannot ever advance you
To the next level—
That you were destined to.
Many accept and endure…
The world that we were born into,
The world that we only know.
But I cannot help seeking all of the answers
For the ultimately unknown
In another world that we do not know,
Yet has to simply exist—
Just as you or I.
Imagine…
If we were only light
And shine on in others' lives,
That we are the ones to leave behind
A greater image of ourselves,
To perfect an even greater mankind!

Shelly Marie Gambino
North Liberty, IN

A Pine for All Seasons

Pine trees majestic, awe-inspiring view,
Spring's fresh green growth infusing renewal.
Several more inches at the branch's end,
Not long from now the colors will blend.

Oh, the pleasant scent from the strong pines,
Furthering the enjoyment of relaxing times.
The spring pines announce the year's beginning,
In winter they're a part of Christmas trimmings.

A tender blend of colors constructing the pine,
Dull grayish hue for a strong, handsome spine.
Bright, verdant needles decorating the branches,
Masculine, yet in the wind they perform dances.

Fallen pine needles create a carpeted ground,
A contrast in color, a soft, calming brown.
In winter their branches hold puffs of white snow,
A pleasing view surely, your mind will take hold.

A stand of pine trees will hinder the wind,
Deer taking refuge, as pines protect them.
While wandering through a pine forest one day,
Peace and serenity will lure you to stay.

Phillip F. Pigeon
Redford, MI

Into Each Life

An old adage claims that
April showers bring May flowers.
Apparently, that conventional wisdom is true.
After today, I think we need a new maxim
stating that May rain storms bring
downed daffodils, toppled tulips,
and magnitudes of magnolia tree blossoms
heaped in drifts upon our sidewalk.

I shoveled away the slick botanical debris
insuring the safety of people walking
to our front door and preventing the tracking
of the morbid mess into our house.
The beauty of each petal, however,
(delicately designed in cream, pink and lavender)
did not elude my eyes; nor did the fragrance
of the tree escape the air I breathed.

Many years ago, the poet Longfellow
pondered a stormy day and penned the words,
"Into each life some rain must fall,
Some days must be dark and dreary."
With that thought, I finished my task,
thankful for the beauty of the tree,
knowing all blossoms eventually fall,
and anticipating the many blooms to come.

David Mayer Gradwohl
Ames, IA

I Saw a Stranger

I saw a stranger walking down the street
and asked him if he wanted something to eat.
And he said thank you ma'am you are so kind
I said I didn't mind.
He was such an old man
so I do what I can.
I asked him if he had a home or place to live,
So I said I have one to give.
He looked at me with tears in his eyes
and said ma'am what a surprise.
I gave him all I had
and he was so glad.
He went into my home with a smile on his face
and bowed his head and said the grace.
He sat at the table with food in his plate
and oh how he ate.
He was tired and needed to rest
It all turned out for the best.
He was no bother
'cause he was my father.

Icie Winters
Shawnee, OK

Some Passes

Impolitic
   The genius of falling acorns
   from trees, autumn's bramble
   and acajou mahogany, and
   orange leaves of Japanese maple.
Evaluating
   Improbable mathematics and
   completing, at time formerly, in
   prospects of all rectifications of
   customers' passbooks.
Saints
   Searching for own standing
   among earlier striding,
   when bereft, of dated and
   independent variants.
Objectives
   Riddled and sheared, one's
   divine economy to be
   Rhoda and Shem, and a
   congruity set of morals.

Patricia Senkaylar
Staten Island, NY

Scarecrow

Does the farmer know what happens after the sun sets?
The scarecrow knows.

After the humans go to bed
Those troublesome boys will see to it
That someone is going to lose their head

The oldest goes over to the pumpkin patch
The scarecrow cannot close his eyes
As the boy brings down the hatchet
The scarecrow cannot tune out the cries

The youngest with lighter in hand
The scarecrow cannot say a word
The boy thinks that the fire is so grand
The scarecrow cannot be heard

The flames trapped the sleeping people
Slowly it begins to devour
Too late to be saved by the townspeople

The townspeople wondered, who murdered the family of three?
The scarecrow knows.

Michelle Strauch
Cassville, MO

Touching You

Every time I see you
I'm totally breathless.
The beauty in your eyes
constantly warms my soul.
The beauty of your face
brings me infinite joy.
The softness of your skin
constantly calls for my touch.
Kissing you softly nourishes my spirit,
but always leaves me hungry for more.
The feel of your heartbeat
keeps my love constant and true.
When you whisper my name,
I go to a place sweeter than Heaven.
I want this slow, delicious dance between us
to last forever.
Holding you gently in my arms
is always my true home.
This is me always touching you.

John Mark Tolbert
Savannah, GA

I love my family clearly. But what's more important is I like them because they're really cool. Being in this country is truly a blessing, so respect the fact that people all over the world want freedom. As for women, think of them as a never-ending adventure. Respect the fact that each one brings a unique perspective to the table of life. Put your hand out and ask them to help you become a better man in all things, and if they put their hand in yours, consider it a start and a blessing.

A Forest Encounter

As I sat upon a stump,
There came a quiet *thump, thump, thump.*
I looked but nothing did I see,
Until a dwarf looked back at me.
"What are you doing there?" said I.

Then angrily came his reply:
"You're sitting on my house, you know!
Get off, get off, get off and go!"

"I'm sorry, sir, I apologize.
Your house? I did not realize.
When on this stump I sat me down, I saw nobody else around.
Had I known it was your home,
I would have left this stump alone."

"The damages," he cried, "are done!
You have awakened the children, every one!
And as you sat yourself right down, you jolted furnishings
    all around!"

"Please, hold your temper little man.
I'll make amends, gladly, if I can!"

When next I turned, the dwarf was gone.
The only thing left was the stump I sat on.
Was this episode only a dream?
Oh, but how real to me it seemed!
If one day you should find my stump and you hear a quiet *thump,
    thump, thump,*
My advice to you is do not stay, but be quickly on your way!

Candace Jean Mosier-McHenry
Bloomsburg, PA

Five Broken Hearts

In front of their small home they stood,
Not knowing what to say,
Their soldier-dad leaves today
To a land at war, far away.

The soldier and his young wife,
A fine young son of four,
Two girls eight and ten;
Dad's going off to war.

Still silence filled the morning air,
The taxi soon would come.
They alone would stay behind,
Alone, the kids and Mum.

Bravado gave way to heartbreak,
Bitter tears fell on the ground;
Deep pain filled all their souls,
Young hearts broke, all around.

The vision still remains,
Two daughters off to school,
Hand in hand and up the street,
To learn the Golden Rule.

Now a lifetime later,
The tears have gone away,
But the moment long remembered
Still breaks their hearts today.

Jerald Christian Bangerter
Kaneohe, HI

The author served his country in Vietnam from 1967 to 1968 and 1972 to 1973. He is a veteran of both the North Vietnamese TET offensive, which started late in the evening of January 30, 1968, and the 1972 April offensive from March 30, 1972, until January 28, 1973. His wife and three children remained in their new rental home in a new city and a new state, hopefully awaiting his return.

Before We Met

Before you,
There must have been a sunny day,
Even one romantic night
Scarred by the Milky Way.
Before you,
There must have been someone,
I must have kissed a tender cheek.
Before you,
I must have tried to share my life,
Thought I found the perfect wife.
Before you,
There must have been a golden moment,
A point in time I tagged with sentiment.
Before you,
I must have dreamt, desired
A trustee for my fragile emotions.
Before you,
I must have lived,
There must have been something... anything
Before you, my love,
I must have loved.
I rummage the archives of my capacity,
Even for the fading stains of a fond memory...
I find nothing.
Seems I have loved only you,
Even before we met.

Floyd J. Thomas
Hartford, CT

The Badge of Courage

Men and women from all walks of life
Enter into service to protect this great land.
The red, white, and blue flies freely in the wind
But at what cost...

These men and women give it their all
To keep this land free, but not without
Their blood pouring over the ground.

Their lives for our freedom
Just doesn't seem right.
They wear their badge of courage
Proudly, for all to see.

Yet we look the other way
When they come home
And don't care
That they are missing limbs or that their lives are in
Shambles.

These proud soldiers gave us our freedom.
Now it's our turn to give back.
Let us say *thank you*
And salute that badge of courage!

Deb Alpaugh
Turbotville, PA

Index of Poets